THE GREAT FRUIT INSPECTOR

Yours in the Truth,
Steve Carney

STEVE CARNEY

Pleasant Word
A Division of WINEPRESS PUBLISHING

© 2008 by Steve Carney. All rights reserved.

Pleasant Word (a division of WinePress Publishing, PO Box 428, Enumclaw, WA 98022) functions only as book publisher. As such, the ultimate design, content, editorial accuracy, and views expressed or implied in this work are those of the author.

No part of this publication may be reproduced, stored in a retrieval system, or transmitted in any way by any means—electronic, mechanical, photocopy, recording, or otherwise—without the prior permission of the copyright holder, except as provided by USA copyright law.

Unless otherwise noted, all Scriptures are taken from the *Holy Bible, New International Version®, NIV®*. Copyright © 1973, 1978, 1984 by the International Bible Society. Used by permission of Zondervan. All rights reserved.

Scripture references marked KJV are taken from the King James Version of the Bible.

Scripture references marked NASB are taken from the New American Standard Bible, © 1960, 1963, 1968, 1971, 1972, 1973, 1975, 1977 by The Lockman Foundation. Used by permission.

ISBN 13: 978-1-4141-0946-6
ISBN 10: 1-4141-0946-6
Library of Congress Catalog Card Number: 2007921456

TABLE OF CONTENTS

Foreword v
Preface ix
Acknowledgments xv
Introduction xvii

Chapter 1: The Purpose and Authority of This Book,
    God's Warning to Man 19
Chapter 2: Why God's Love Brings Judgment 31
Chapter 3: Judging the Fruit of Righteousness 81
Chapter 4: Cleansing an Unhealthy Body 135
Chapter 5: Judgment of Rulers, *The Rise and Fall of Kings* 177
Chapter 6: Judgments for Nations, *Speak to the Nations* 203
Chapter 7: The Final Chapter, *What Is Your Part?* 229

Appendix 1: The Truth Will Make You Free! 239
Appendix 2: The Truth Will Make You Free! 241
Endnotes 245

FOREWORD

Dear Reader:

Do these two things before reading this wonderful book:

1. Buckle your safety harness for the ride of your life, as you effortlessly flow through one after another of these marvelous vignettes, which demonstrate the spiritual principles of wisdom, faith, and becoming intimately acquainted with the Great Fruit Inspector.
2. Comb your hair and brush your teeth, because you are going to meet your Master in these Bible-laden pages.

Reverend Carney has drawn upon the Word of God, his own personal experiences, and extensive biblical research to produce a blockbuster of a book. His writing is effective in bringing the timeless verses of ancient Holy Writ into relevant treatment of the most urgent issues in our real-life world of conflict, pride, and rebellion against our Maker. His pertinent illustrations have brightened my day and renewed my faith that a life of grace and mercy is not only possible, but is indeed attainable, by those who will walk in holiness and the fear of the Lord.

This book reveals the truth of the judgment of God, with a distinct and profound emphasis upon the boundless love of the Almighty. It is written as though the author were actually acquainted with the Great God of the Ages. Reverend Carney refers not only to Job and Saint Paul, but also to Albert Einstein. His gift of drawing from the entire landscape of pertinent references lends an authenticity to the book that no amount of editing, ghost-writing, or book-doctoring could ever have achieved.

The author's many years of ministry, including leading in-depth study groups on the God Chasers (with his wife Gabriela and his son Mario), and working in the Sunday School Cell Ministry of Victory Christian Center, Tulsa, Oklahoma, have qualified him to write on these powerful topics of timely significance. He also works many hours behind the scenes, preparing classrooms for the hundreds of people who attend Sunday School each week. "Faithful" is written indelibly across the expanse of his lifetime of service to the Lord and to hurting humanity. I saw him and his family sweating profusely while loading many huge tractor-trailers with food, water, and supplies for the victims of Hurricane Katrina.

What is the purpose of this book? To impress upon us the seriousness of the human predicament at this stage in history, when all will be judged, and those who have repented of sin will be delivered from the wrath of God's righteousness. It is to call all of us to move swiftly away from our wicked prejudices and self-centered thoughtlessness and toward the desired state of having the love of God shed abroad, from our hearts, to all the inhabitants of the earth.

This book will make an important contribution to your understanding of these topics. In fact, it has implications for the entire world of Christendom, which has been occasionally accused of easy-believism. At times the accusations have had some merit in actual fact, and at times the Church has been maligned. At any rate, the message of this book is we must clean up our own house so the hordes of lost pilgrims will come to know there is a refuge of righteousness, to which they may freely turn, "IF THEY REPENT AND TURN FROM THEIR WICKED WAYS." The Church, as the extension of the heart of the Savior, must maintain its own purity, in order to be available for satisfying the extensive love-hunger of a contentious world.

Steve Carney's use of language is easily understandable and engaging. The active voice from which he speaks is obviously God-breathed and Spirit-inspired. Now, turn the page, and let the wisdom of God speak into your spirit.

Have a happy day!
Cal Easterling, Ph.D., Sunday School Superintendent
Victory Christian Center, Tulsa, Oklahoma

PREFACE

This book was not written out of self-ambition, to make a name for myself. I do not covet fame or a television ministry. My greatest prize is to fellowship with the One who created me. If the cares of a huge ministry would keep me from my desire, I want no part of it, nor fame, nor the adoration of huge crowds.

My favorite activity is time spent in intercessory prayer. I also enjoy quiet meditation, walking nature trails in national parks, listening to birds, breathing fresh air. For during these times alone, God's presence comes in such a sweet, tangible way.

This book will not explain or debate pre-tribulation, post-tribulation, or any other issues concerning the end times. The primary objective of this book is also not to encourage, although you will be encouraged if you heed its warnings, but I seek to reveal the truth, concerning God's judgment. We must remember His judgment is not given out of hate, because God is not mean or hateful. He doesn't wait to catch us breaking His commandments. God is love, and He judges the earth to bring about peace, deliverance, and salvation. Yes, God does get angry at sin and rebellion, because it results in death. Nevertheless, His driving motive is love.

X • THE GREAT FRUIT INSPECTOR

Judgment has always carried a bad connotation, as though God were evil for bringing it about. As a matter of fact, the opposite is true. God is not willing that any should perish, but wishes for all to come to repentance, so His judgment is consequently good. It is necessary to protect the righteous and save mankind from total annihilation. As we shall see, judgment brings about justice, righteousness, and order, which will bring about the utopia for which mankind has craved since the fall of Adam and Eve.

Man's judgment is flawed, but God's judgment is perfect. Since His wisdom is far above men, most people do not understand His judgments. With the help of God's Word, as revealed by the Holy Spirit, we will tap into some of the wisdom behind His judgments.

This message is not intended to condemn, but to bring freedom. I am no judge, having stubbornly rebelled in the past. I realize how I would have destroyed myself had it not been for God's mercy. But He has made the decision to give man the ability to rule his own life. Even shortly before this book was published, God revealed many areas of my life which still needed adjusting, lest I be lifted with pride and self-righteousness.

In the book of Job, Eliphaz, one of Job's friends, asked the question,

> What is man, that he could be pure, or one born of woman, that he could be righteous?
>
> —Job 15:14

I tremble as I realize the responsibility of one claiming to speak for God, so my deepest concern is misrepresenting his character. Jesus taught with gentleness and meekness and only showed anger when confronting hypocritical religious leaders of the day. He also had stern rebukes in His letters to the churches of Asia, recorded in the book of Revelation.

Because of the nature of this subject, I do not have the time or space to present the gentle side of our Savior, as I would like. However, the vast majority of books in the Christian market already address God's love and prosperity, but this one reveals the stern side of the Master, the side we will see when He comes in power and great glory, to judge all nations. By understanding both, the Holy Spirit can bring the Church into balance. He desires God's people to know truth and to humbly receive correction, rather than to continually avoid his rebuke, which only proves He loves us, as Revelation 3:19 says.

Thank God we are still alive in this period of grace, when He lets us repent, receive forgiveness of sin, and receive Christ as Lord. As we shall see, God's Spirit will not always strive with man, even in this present day period of grace.

I've felt it appropriate to address the evil reasoning and imaginations prevalent in our entire society, rather than only in individuals. After all, we don't really fight people, but against principalities of darkness, who plant twisted thoughts and reasoning within the hearts of men. But we also know men will be held accountable for rejecting Christ and for yielding to evil. The Word of God will judge, and the Holy Spirit will convict us of sin, so this book reveals God's judgment motivated by love, to give us mercy.

A second purpose is to instill a healthy fear and respect for God. Our generation has rebelled and formed a disrespectful attitude of lawlessness toward God's commandments. Yet Jesus is the Word. Therefore, to disrespect His commandments is to dishonor Him. We show our love and respect by obeying God's Word.

I noticed in many old hymns of the eighteenth and nineteenth centuries, even pronouns referring to the Godhead are capitalized. Thereupon, I felt it proper to search this book and capitalize all references to the Godhead. This does not imply Christian authors who do not capitalize God's pronouns think of Him with less respect. God will be feared among the nations, and we will see it in our generation.

Third, I want to give a wakeup call. Toward the end of the twentieth century, the Holy Spirit revealed to me how the Church had gotten out of balance. We have failed to emphasize truth concerning repentance, judgment, holiness, and the discipline of the Lord. Therefore, the spirit of lawlessness has exploded, even affecting the saints. God, through the prayers of His saints, will stem this tide and usher in His great and final harvest.

Finally, I hope to help us prepare for the coming of the Lord. The truth is, even if the Messiah didn't return during this generation to rule upon the earth, every one of us will face death. Every man who ever lived will one day face Him individually, at Judgment, and give account of his life. What is your part in these end times, and how can you get ready for His coming?

At the end of each chapter are thoughts to ponder how the subject applies to you, as an individual. Also, there are questions to help you search your heart. These are practical steps to apply truths to your life.

Since judgments have already begun to increase and will continue to increase at a faster pace in the coming decades, it is essential to explain this subject with authority. What is a higher authority than the Bible? Since few books deal with judgment and discipline, most of the examples and illustrations are taken from the Word of God, for validity. The book is filled with Scripture. God's Word is my final authority. According to Hebrews 4:12, the Word is living, sharper than a two-edged sword, dividing the soul from the spirit. So I admonish you to meditate on the scriptures quoted in these pages. God will also give you revelation and understanding from them.

A revival is coming. Like a mighty wave, I believe it will gain momentum. Now in its infancy, this revival will bring a great harvest of precious souls. Our Lord has been waiting for this time with great patience. We have already seen the beginning of it, with the utilization of satellites and the fall of the Iron Curtain. This revival will continue building momentum, until the work on earth is done. The Church of Jesus Christ must make the necessary sacrifices and take bold steps of faith.

The prophecy of Jesus that His gospel will be preached to every tongue, tribe, and nation shall be fulfilled though many who are to witness this great revival will later pass from the scene. Afterwards, there will be a falling away once again into lawlessness. New generations will forget God and return to lawlessness, deceived by the Antichrist. This will be the time of great judgment and tribulations.

God is waiting for us, His precious fruit, people of His earth, not willing any should perish. He awaits His Church to arise in this final hour and take hold of destiny. We must realize the urgency of this hour and boldly step into God's plan for our lives. As gross darkness and judgment fills the earth, this can be the Church's finest hour. Will we recognize it and seize the moment? Will we be ready and willing—before the great judgment?

ACKNOWLEDGMENTS

This book is sent out as an offering of sacrifice, unto the God who inspired its pages. God made writing this book possible. I humbly give thanks unto Him, the revealer of all truth, who has chosen the weak to confound the wise. There is no end to His truth. It shall stand forever. To Him who sits on the throne and to the Lamb be power, blessing, honor and glory, now and forever.

I also express gratitude to my wife and son, who patiently sacrificed their time, without husband and father, so I could pen these words for the glory of God. My wife was there to encourage, to love and to support. Thanks for believing in my dreams.

Also, to my siblings and especially Mom, whom I left years ago to begin this journey of faith. I remember the tears of my mother as I drove away in obedience to God. It has now been more than twenty years since I took a step of faith and left my precious family. I have not been able to be near mom very much, during the sunset of her life, but God has provided faithful brothers and sisters to look after her. Thank you for honoring our mom. You will receive rewards in this life, as well as in the life to come.

I am grateful to Sandra and Terry Clifton, who introduced me to the world of publishing. You convinced me I could really publish a book. Also, thanks to Reba McBride, who later took over the Writer's Workshop class.

Many thanks to Dr. Cal Easterling for quiet, yet confident leadership. Your positive attitude and love for people kept me from getting into a ditch—theologically. You are extremely intelligent, yet you are humble enough to relate to common people.

Thanks to Leslie Sims and the Sunday school at Victory Christian Center in Tulsa, for being a good base of spiritual support.

I'd like to commend the pastors of my local church here in Tulsa, for protecting God's sheep from ravenous wolves. Thank you to the pastors, youth leaders, Sunday school teachers, and Vacation Bible School teachers of the Southern Baptist churches I attended as a child. You imparted to me the love of God, a love for people, and a hatred for evil.

Thanks to all the teachers at Rhema Bible Training Center during the time I attended, 1986-1988. You imparted to me the Spirit of Faith. Without faith, I couldn't have completed this project.

Finally, thank you to my editor Penny Lent for fine-tuning this book. You added a touch of scholarly elegance, while making the book reader friendly. Also to Joseph Ellis, George Dillaway, Athena Dean, Abigail Davidson, and all the staff at Winepress Publishing, thank you for your courteous and professional service. You have demonstrated a servant's heart.

To all who helped me in the past, thank you for showing me mercy.

Yours in the Truth,
Steve Carney

INTRODUCTION

As clouds begin to darken the distant sky before a coming storm, the age of judgment can be seen on our horizon. Foreshadowing includes the tragedy at Waco, Texas; the bombing in Oklahoma City, OK; terrorist attacks on the twin towers in New York City and at the Pentagon, in Virginia; a terrible tsunami, which took thousands of lives in the Far East; Hurricane Katrina in Gulf Coast American states; fighting in the Middle East. The list of catastrophes goes on and on. As tragedies intensify—like a woman's birth pains—each calamity is a warning: Caution. Danger Ahead. Warning. Rebellion is hazardous to your health. Beware the soul that sins, it shall die. Detour. Change direction in your life.

As these disasters continue to occur, people ask many questions:

> Are these tragedies the result of God judging the earth?
> If God is love, why does He allow injustice, pain, and sorrow?
> How and why does God bring judgment?
> How can we escape God's judgment?

XVIII • THE GREAT FRUIT INSPECTOR

At the same time, the light of God's kingdom is getting brighter on the horizon, like the breaking of dawn: The gospel is going forth into all nations. God does reveal Himself more and more, through Jesus Christ. More Christian communication goes around the globe than ever before. Christians in many countries stand for moral principals and challenge the status quo.

Many believers in the Church also ask questions:

How do we stand up to the evils of society, without being judgmental?
Why do Christians suffer?
Are the Ten Commandments relevant for today?
What is the role of discipline in the Church?
Is the coming of Christ near?

The Great Fruit Inspector provides answers to these questions. There are very few books on the Christian market that deal with the controversial subject of God's judgment. This book was written with answers, based on the declaration that the Bible is the inspired Word of God.

If you doubt the Bible, you will probably doubt the contents of this book. If you believe the Bible is God speaking to man, you will hold a healthy respect for the words of this book.

The Great Fruit Inspector contains many stories from the Bible. Indeed, it is divine revelation, based on the Bible. It is a prophetic warning for today's generation.

Chapter 1

THE PURPOSE AND AUTHORITY OF THIS BOOK
GOD'S WARNING TO MAN

It was a rainy, dreary Tuesday morning as Stella Snowden sat at the breakfast table, reading the newspaper. Occasionally, the thunder rattled the house like a large explosion. Stella had a sleepless night, worrying about her son, who was stationed in Iraq. She had a spirit of heaviness. *I hope my son is okay*, she thought to herself. She couldn't seem to keep her mind on the news. As she sat at the table drinking dark roasted coffee, there was a knock at the door.

When she opened the door, two young men stood in uniform with large gray overcoats. With sober faces, they stood straight and tall in a most stately manner, oblivious to the rain pelting their caps and shoulders. "Mrs. Snowden," one of the young men addressed her in a serious voice, as if to confirm her identity

"Yes?" she replied in a strained tone of anxiety.

"I'm Sergeant Michael Blake, with the United States Army. May we come in?" he asked, his voice softening with compassion.

Suddenly, a cloud of dread descended upon her, as the young men entered into the living room, shutting the front door behind them.

His crystal blue eyes of compassion peering into hers, the young soldier wasted no time, breaking the news as gently as he possibly could, "Mrs. Snowden, I deeply regret to inform you, your son was killed in action last night, as he participated in a raid on insurgent forces."

Her tears began to flow, like the rain outside. During the next few weeks Stella's grief turned to anger. She looked at her son's most recent photo; his red hair, freckled face, and cheerful countenance. Though she was raised in a Christian family and often attended church services, she questioned God, "Why didn't you protect my son? Why did you allow this to happen?"

Jason returned to inspect his house after a devastating hurricane. He and his wife had worked hard to save money for a down payment and a new life in the suburbs of Kenner, Louisiana. Now, after diligent work and several promotions, it was finally a reality—a beautiful brick and cypress structure.

This quality house should last the rest of my life. I should be able to retire in this home, Jason had thought, comfortable and pleased at his wise investment.

Four bedrooms and two baths provided plenty of breathing room for their family of five. It was a stark contrast to the tiny, three-bedroom home they had recently moved from, just a few miles from the city of New Orleans. And this neighborhood was much farther outside of New Orleans, Louisiana. The bedrooms were all located upstairs. Downstairs was a modern kitchen, dining room, den for recreation, an office, and a spacious living room. In addition to the large living area, they had a three-car garage.

Jason's heart sank as he drove up to his new home that day. Immediately noticeable were massive amounts of wind damage and mud. As he stepped inside what was left of his family home, he smelled mold and mildew from the flood. He spent the next few weeks trying to salvage personal possessions. Finally, because of water damage, his home had to be razed to the ground and totally rebuilt.

As a believer in Christ, he lived by the prosperity message and had sowed finances in his church and many ministries. So he trusted God to provide the money and grace to rebuild. Thank God, he did have homeowner's insurance. Even so, he couldn't help but wonder, *Why did God allow this to happen?*

Amar was a devoted Muslim. He tried hard to please Allah. He tried to do all that was required of the Muslim faith. He was a good father to his children. Yet he feared Allah's anger. Amar owned a small fishing boat and fish market on the beach, in his country of Sri Lanka. Some of his fish were exported to Calcutta, India. He worked hard to provide for his family.

One beautiful, bright morning he and his workers sailed out to fish, while the warm sun glistened on the white-capped ocean. Perhaps Allah would prosper his efforts today. Then an unusual, almost eerie stillness surrounded them. Where were the seagulls that usually followed, waiting for a chance to steal their catch of fish? Gradually, a great undercurrent began to pull their boat out to sea. They apprehensively struggled to keep from drifting.

In the distance they noticed a wave approaching. As it drew closer, Amar realized it was no ordinary wave; as it raced forward, he became paralyzed with fear. The swell lifted the boat high and propelled it toward shore. The crew helplessly clung to the sides, as if for their very lives. After only minutes, they were abruptly beached. Amar stood, aghast at the debris and bodies littering the shoreline, giving realization to the magnitude of destruction.

Then his thoughts turned toward his wife and children, *Did they survive?* He rushed home but found nothing but destruction. Their small bamboo home had totally disappeared! His meager fish market was also gone. Amar waited in agony, for three weeks, before he learned his wife and three of his children had perished in the tsunami. Only one ten-year-old son was spared. Though overcome with grief and sadness, Amar had no choice but to pick up the broken pieces of his life and start over. He mentally asked, *What sins have I done against Allah to bring this upon my family?*

These are a few examples out of thousands of daily personal tragedies, all over the world. As a result of recent catastrophes, people everywhere, of all faiths, are asking serious questions: Are these tragedies the result of God judging the earth? If God is love, why does He allow injustice, pain, and sorrow? How and why does God bring judgment? How can we escape? Are we approaching the end of the age? The following chapters in this book provide biblical answers, which ring with the authority of divine inspiration.

You may ask, "Who is this author? How can he make such claims?"

This book began shortly before the 21st Century, as we approached a new millennium, when God began stirring in my heart. The Holy Spirit impressed upon me that judgments would increase in the 21st century. While I received no specifics about what, when, and where, I sensed in my heart that more tragedies were soon to occur which would make a lasting impact on this generation. I began to sense the urgency of the times. No longer would the everyday life of going to work, paying bills, and shallow entertainment be acceptable. God had instilled within me a zeal to redeem the time here on earth, and my life would never be the same.

I first received this zeal when I was anointed by the Holy Ghost, on the Day of Pentecost, in 1983. This anointing gave me a special grace to pray for all nations. For the remaining decade, I spent frequent time in prayer, until the fall of the Iron Curtain and the Soviet Empire. After the fall of the communist governments in Europe, I gradually grew spiritually dull and lazy. The zeal I once had faded somewhat, and I found myself discontent and bored with life, during the 1990s. However, God would not let me forever drift away in lethargy.

Fifteen years later, shortly before the 21st Century, God began stirring in my heart again. He first showed me how the spirit of lawlessness had increased, not only in the world, but even in the church. He then revealed future judgments to come upon the earth: An increase in the intensity of earthquakes; an increased number and intensity of storms; an increase in droughts, famine, and disease; an increased number and intensity of fires; an increase in the general temperature of the earth. All these are beginning signs, pointing to the end of the age and the second coming of Christ.

God revealed how spiritual laws affect natural laws, and how the increase of these natural and man-made disasters coincide with the increase in lawlessness. People remember when Comet Shoemaker-Levy 9 collided with Jupiter during the 1990s. During its orbit around Jupiter, the comet was broken apart by tidal forces into at least 21 pieces. These pieces continued to orbit Jupiter for approximately two years before the first piece impacted the planet on July 16, 1994. Other pieces of the comet followed until the last piece slammed into Jupiter on July 22, 1994. This astronomical phenomenon was not without spiritual significance. Pictures were broadcast showing the breathtaking sight. That massive collision was one of many signs signaling the approaching end of the age, on God's flawless timetable.

Jesus spoke, in the twenty-fourth chapter of Matthew, about signs in the sun, moon, and stars. There will be more signs in the heavens before the Son of Man returns. These signs are frightening, terrible, and awesome. Jesus said men's hearts would fail because of fear when they see these awful things coming upon the earth.

Jesus also told His disciples, "When these things begin to occur, look up, for your redemption draws near" (Luke 21:28).

For the Church, there will be a mighty outpouring of His glory as the Great Tribulation period draws near. People of God will continue to grow in the knowledge of God. Some will amaze the world with mighty works of the Holy Spirit. They will walk in true holiness, their garments white, washed in the blood of the Lamb. And their light will grow brighter and brighter, bringing in the great final harvest.

The authority of this book, *The Great Fruit Inspector*, comes not from my reputation. At this time, I am not well known by men. The authority of this book is derived from scriptures, which support it. The Bible is God speaking to men. *The Great Fruit Inspector* is written, based on the Bible. God has ordained these words.

Understanding principles in this book will give God the respect, honor, and glory He deserves. He is still in control, and all the nations will know He is God. God doesn't simply suggest, but commands us to reverence Him.

One of my greatest desires is for men everywhere to hear the words of God and be delivered from darkness. If you will recognize the authority given to me, for the purpose of writing *The Great Fruit Inspector*, you will be able to receive understanding from God. If you heed and do the scriptures quoted in this book, you will be delivered from darkness into His light. If you do not take lightly the warnings of this book, you will be prosperous and have good success.

How can I make such claims? Because the truths of *The Great Fruit Inspector* are taken directly from the Bible. His Spirit bears witness of His inspired truth and revelation. If you are born again, you have the Spirit of Truth within you. Therefore, judge the words of this book, whether they are from God.

Each person born into the earth has a unique, heavenly destiny and purpose. God has given each person natural gifts to glorify God and benefit others. Our natural gifts may be in childcare, music, art, business, or some other natural ability. Those born into the body of Christ also have spiritual gifts such as prayer, giving, service, administration, or some other spiritual gift mentioned in the Bible. It is our responsibility to find our purpose in life and, with God's help, fulfill it.

In May of 1983, on the Day of Pentecost, God radically changed my life. He anointed me and gave me authority for the purpose to which I have been called. When He speaks and ordains, it will come to pass. I realized the gifts He places on His children were not for us to live boring, shallow, fruitless lives. God is not wasteful. He doesn't save and anoint us simply so we can aimlessly waste our lives with the weights and cares of the world.

So there I was, approaching middle age, as well as the turn of the century, and yet doing nothing about the work God had assigned for me! But our faithful, unchanging God began to stir my spirit, and it got stronger every day. I felt like the prophet Jeremiah, when he refused to prophesy because of the persecution; only, I refused because of unbelief and selfishness.

I suppose I acted more like the prophet Jonah, who ran from God and was swallowed up in the belly of a fish. I tried to stay in my comfort zone, afraid to launch God's work, but his Word was like a fire, burning in my bones. I felt compelled to release the Word of the Lord, lest I explode. I felt constrained to tell someone what the Holy Spirit was revealing! I needed to convince someone of the urgent times in which we are living.

Since I was not a minister, I surmised my family was the only audience I had to share what God had revealed to me. With this in mind, I wrote my brother, sisters, nieces, and nephews a letter. This simple letter is in the first appendix of this book.

However, I began to doubt what God was showing me. *Maybe this is Satan trying to put negative thoughts in my mind.* Neglecting my prayer life, I refused to surrender to the leading of the Holy Spirit. When I sensed the importance of the message and magnitude of the events which were about to occur, I tried to hide in my comfort zone. Deep inside, I knew I was running from what God wanted me to do.

I fully intended this letter to be the first and last one. Afterwards, I again became busy with the cares of the world and tried to forget about it. But my careless choices led me outside of God's divine protection. It was only because of God's unending mercy that I was not totally destroyed.

About two years later, shortly before the tragedy of September 11, 2001, God again arrested my attention. Subsequent to 9/11, I had resumed writing monthly letters on a consistent basis, and the revelations from God again began to flow. I began sending these letters to several well-known ministries and leaders. The first letter after 9/11 is found in the second appendix of this book. After that, God revealed a clearer perspective on things to come.

My remarkable adventure of revelation had begun. After about two years of writing monthly letters, the revelation was coming so quickly, the letters couldn't contain it. I felt the Holy Spirit leading me to write a book. He gave me grace to complete what He had begun. Such a seemingly insignificant act of faith as writing letters had turned into a journey with destiny. At the time, I had little idea where God was taking me. So I finally decided to take a

THE PURPOSE AND AUTHORITY OF THIS BOOK • 27

small step of obedience, and He did the rest. Much of this book is taken from those letters.

As with everyone who steps out to obey God, this book has been a journey of faith, with many obstacles to overcome. The process of penning these words has taken about five years, though some of the thoughts had been birthed in my spirit many years before I put them into writing. A few of these truths came to me during the 1980s. These were truths which, to my knowledge, few preached at the time.

As the title suggests, this is a unique book, which dares to seek answers for difficult questions. Scriptures, using the principals of homiletics, support every concept discussed. Many years of thought and research were put into *The Great Fruit Inspector*. At one period, there was a seven or eight-month interruption before I could resume writing. But its completion is living proof that through faith and patience, we inherit the promises of God, as stated in Hebrews 6:12.

Though I am an imperfect being, I believe the Spirit of God within inspired the ideas and wisdom for this book. I can say, as Mel Gibson said of his famous movie, *The Passion of the Christ*, this book may be the purpose for which I was born.

It is up to you, who have the Spirit of God within, to judge its contents and determine whether God inspired it.

FRUIT INSPECTION

In Chapter 1, what did God reveal to the author that started this book and will lead to coming judgments upon the earth?

_____

_____

_____

_____

What is the primary claim to support the author's authority? List other claims that support the authority of *The Great Fruit Inspector*:

The scriptures

3. What can you learn from the author's testimony about making the most of your time here on the earth?

4. Why were his letters significant in writing this book?

5. What's the primary purpose of *The Great Fruit Inspector*?

6. Does God ever get angry?

Yes, God does get angry at sin and rebellion because it results in death.

Pg 1

Exodus 22:24:

Numbers 18:5:

Deuteronomy 1:37:

Luke 14:21:

Mark 3:5:

Revelation 6:16

7. Why is God's judgment sometimes necessary?
   _____
   _____
   _____
   _____

8. What does God's judgment produce?
   _____
   _____
   _____
   _____

9. Why does Jesus rebuke His people in Revelation 20:11?
   _____
   _____
   _____
   _____

10. Why does God wait, before He sends final judgments upon the earth, in James 5:7?
    _____
    _____
    _____
    _____

CHAPTER 2

WHY GOD'S LOVE BRINGS JUDGMENT

During these recent, sobering times, many people ask relevant questions. Why does God allow tragic events? Why doesn't God protect our nation? Why are all of these bad things happening to my family and to me?

Yet I urge you to stay in the love of God. Always remember, God is good and the devil is bad. God does good works. The devil does evil works. God is love. Satan is hate. Love triumphs over hate. Meditation on the love of God is a necessity, as the end of the age approaches and judgments increase.

Our frustration is we know God is love, so how can He be love and yet allow such tragedies to occur? How does God's love and judgment relate?

Jesus was God manifested in the flesh, and He lived the perfect life of love. At no time in His life on earth do we see him destroy, only heal. At the same time, He did pronounce judgment on the Pharisees, on Capernaum where He spent the major portion of His ministry, and on Jerusalem for rejecting Him as king.

Some believe God could never allow judgment that resulted in destruction. There are some who even refuse to believe there is a hell, and that anyone will go there. Yet, the Bible makes it clear; the God of love has prepared a Lake of Fire for Satan and the fallen angels. Moreover, many will be condemned to the eternal Lake of Fire. God destroyed the men of Noah's generation in a flood. He also destroyed Sodom. Likewise, He destroyed the Egyptian army in the Red Sea. But we still ask, how can a God of love allow such things?

There are questions for which we may never find the answers in this life. If God answered some questions, we still may not be able to comprehend them with our limited minds. I do believe the Holy Spirit can answer many questions, if we ask in faith. Let's search the Scriptures together and trust in His Spirit of revelation to find answers.

> Like a fluttering sparrow or a darting swallow, an undeserved curse does not come to rest.
> —Proverbs 26:2

There are several reasons judgments occur. Natural laws in effect can cause judgment; people's poor choices and rebellion also do. God also gives judgments for seeds of evil, and bad incidents also occur because we are at the wrong place at the wrong time. We can be affected by tragedies due to someone else's decision, accidents, and war, such as terrorist activities.

It Rains on the Just and the Unjust

There remains the age-old question Job asked, when going through his horrendous affliction. Why does it sometimes appear the good suffer, while the wicked prosper, as Job 21:7-15 asks? We may never be sure of the answers to all these questions, but the Bible does give us some insight.

Perhaps people who do not know God were, nevertheless, taught sound moral principles at home and at school. Although they do not know God, they can still put these moral principles into practice and begin to prosper.

God sometimes allows the wicked to live a long life because of His mercy. He wants no man to enter into eternal darkness. But death for a righteous man is a promotion into paradise. An early death for righteous men like Stephen, the Apostle James, and other Christian martyrs is not so tragic, when you think of the wonderful life that awaits them.

Perhaps another reason we see a righteous person judged more swiftly than a wicked person is because the righteous are more familiar with the teachings of our Lord. In some cases, they have been taught right from wrong and know better than those who have never been taught the Word of truth.

> That servant who knows his master's will and does not get ready or does not do what his master wants will be beaten with many blows. But the one who does not know and does things deserving punishment will be beaten with few blows. From everyone who has been given much, much will be demanded; and from the one who has been entrusted with much, much more will be asked.
> —Luke 12:47-48

Sometimes, judgment for the wicked will also affect the righteous. For example, those who were killed in the terrible tragedy of 9/11 were affected by terrorists' decisions. In these cases, we must stay in the center of God's will for our lives. In addition, we must also trust in His guidance and divine protection. There are those who love the Lord, but perhaps became too busy to hear His voice or to pray the words of Jesus, "Lead us not into temptation, but deliver us from evil," as in Matthew 6:13.

Natural and spiritual laws affect both the righteous and the unrighteous. So we can understand judgment of the United States, as a nation, will affect all who live in America, the just and the unjust alike.

God judged His people in Judah by allowing the Babylonians to invade and conquer. Even righteous men like Daniel were affected by the judgment of God; he was captured and carried away to Babylonia, in Daniel 1:1-19. Yet, Daniel found favor and rose to the top of the government in a wicked nation. So we see even when God brings judgment to a nation, He will always protect those who fear and obey Him. Daniel was carried off to Babylonia because of the sins of his nation, yet he remained faithful to God.

The prophet Jeremiah was affected by this invasion as well. Jeremiah had to go through the siege of Jerusalem. His own people imprisoned him because he prophesied the truth, but when the Babylonians captured the city, Jeremiah received favor with the captain of their army. The captain insisted Jeremiah come back to Babylonia with him. He promised Jeremiah would be respected and well treated. However, Jeremiah refused the offer, choosing to suffer with the people of God even in their rebellion. According to tradition, this eventually led to his death. So Jeremiah also suffered greatly because of the choice of others.

In the book of Lamentations, Jeremiah weeps in anguish over the captivity of Jerusalem. I think he felt what was in the heart of God. But his own people eventually murdered him, because he refused to remain silent over their wickedness.

Suffering for the Sake of Righteousness

Like the prophet Jeremiah, other godly saints chose hardship, suffering, and even death to glorify God, as revealed in Hebrews, chapter 11. These endured suffering because of their steadfastness in the faith and their stand for righteousness. Jeremiah was one of these heroes of faith.

The author of Hebrews tells of other heroes of faith, who through faith subdued kingdoms, administered righteousness, obtained promises, stopped the mouths of lions, quenched the violence of fire, escaped the edge of the sword, in their weakness became strong, valiant in fight, routed invading armies of foreigners.

Women received their dead, raised to life again. Some believers were tortured, not accepting deliverance, so they might obtain a better resurrection. Others had trials of cruel ridicule and flogging, chains and imprisonment. Believers have been stoned, sawed in two, tempted, and murdered with the sword. They have wandered about in sheepskins and goatskins, destitute, afflicted, and tormented—of whom the world was not worthy. They wandered in deserts, in mountains, and in dens and caves of the earth.

> These were all commended for their faith, yet none of them received what had been promised. God had planned something better for us so that only together with us would they be made perfect.
> —Hebrews 11:39-40

Notice these heroes of faith, who endured such tragedy, obtained a good report through faith. The description of these heroes of faith is hardly one of prosperity. In the world's view, it appeared they failed to obtain wealth and possessions here on earth. Some believers would say these heroes of faith missed the perfect plan of God, by this lack. Some would say they were being judged for their lack of faith, since there is a judgment for the disobedient. I understand, because I have personally known the judgment of disobedience.

Yet, the scriptures indicate these people of God chose to endure affliction for the sake of the truth, a far cry from arrogant disobedience. Indeed, the world was not worthy of them. Furthermore, they did not receive some of God's promises during their lifetime, since they came to pass in future generations. But God had provided something better for them—the hope of a better resurrection.

Jesus also endured this type of suffering. Most of His disciples drank the cup of suffering, as well. Some disciples of Christ may die in an accident or on the battlefield. But whether we live or die, we do so in faith, for the glory of God, trusting in His divine guidance and protection. Many testimonies are recorded throughout history of how saints glorified God in their death, without fear, in peace. They died trusting the faithfulness of God. With joy, they entered death victorious. Indeed, we can't assume everyone who endures hardship or tragedy is being judged for rebellion.

Natural and Spiritual Laws

Throughout the Bible, it is evident how God allows judgment to fall on individuals and nations. If God is such a good God, why does He allow judgment to occur at all? God is not evil, but good. He judges individuals and nations for this exact reason. God's goodness demands He judge the earth. Let's expand on specific reasons why God allows judgment.

First, God's judgment is a result of natural and spiritual laws that He spoke into effect. There must be order in God's universe, to prevent chaos. He is a God of order and perfection, right down to the tiniest atom. Laws of physics include the theory of relativity, the law of inertia, and the law of gravity. For example, gravity keeps objects from floating away. Imagine the chaos on earth if this were not so. There are mathematical laws as well, and grammatical laws for various languages. God's universe is well ordered. From the tiniest part of an atom to the largest star of the universe, all were created with structure and perfect order.

> Your word, O LORD, is eternal; it stands firm in the heavens. Your faithfulness continues through all generations; you established the earth, and it endures. Your laws endure to this day, for all things serve you.
> —Psalms 119:89-91

Occasionally, God will intervene on behalf of those who are in covenant with him and will make exceptions to natural laws. Such was the case of Daniel, who was affected by the sins of his nation and was carried off to Babylonia. God's judgment of Judah caused Daniel to face many trials there. However, he remained faithful to the God of Israel, and God protected him. God intervened when Daniel was thrown into the den of hungry lions for his faith, and an angel shut their mouths.

God can intervene to heal sickness and disease today also. When He intervenes with natural laws on behalf of His people of any age, we call these supernatural miracles.

In the same way as natural laws, God created spiritual laws. For instance, there is the law of sowing and reaping, the law of forgiveness, the law of repentance, the law of faith, the law of love, and the law of judgment. Spiritual laws will always affect natural laws.

The disobedience of Adam and Eve affected the entire universe and set into motion the law of sin and death. Moreover, the obedience of Jesus affected the entire universe, too. He reversed the law of sin and death and set into motion the law of the Spirit of life. So obedience will result in life and disobedience in death.

Similarly, our personal obedience or disobedience will influence others, either positively for the kingdom of God, or negatively for the kingdom of darkness. These are God's spiritual laws. Even as it may take some time for us to see the effects of natural laws, it also takes time for us to see the effects of spiritual laws.

When Adam and Eve disobeyed God, this set into motion the spiritual laws of sin and death. The immediate effect of these spiritual laws was they were thrown out of the Garden of Eden. However, other negative results took effect gradually. Adam and Eve eventually experienced physical death.

The law of sin and death led to the great flood. After the flood, man was forced to till the land to provide food. And now, with the passing of each generation, we see more deadly viruses, germs, and bacteria. As the law of sin and death continues its course, we also see more violence, even from animals. We see greater perversion, anger, and stress.

Only one power can stop and reverse it: Jesus Christ. The shed blood of the innocent Lamb and His resurrection power alone can stop the progression of this terrible law of disobedience, because Christ's work of redemption set into motion the law of the Spirit of life! The immediate effect of new life was evident in Christ's disciples on the Day of Pentecost. His harvest was souls, transformed and delivered. We still see healing and miracles occur. A born-again believer is the greatest miracle of all. They receive a whole new nature and are filled with God's Holy Spirit.

As new creatures in Christ, the law of the Spirit of life sets us free from the law of sin and death. We no longer must offer the sacrifice of bulls and goats, but ourselves, the sacrifice of a broken and contrite spirit. Through godly sorrow, repentance, and faith in the blood of the Lamb, we can receive forgiveness for our sins.

The law of the Spirit of life provides restoration. If we continue in God's word, we can become more like Christ. Through faith in Jesus Christ, we no longer have to fear sickness and death. Under this spiritual law, truth and righteousness prevail. The power of the Spirit of life is far greater than the law of sin and death. The effects of this gift continue to expand and will one day cover the entire earth, when Christ rules from Jerusalem.

THE LAW OF SOWING AND REAPING

As individuals, the effects of spiritual laws within our own lives are often not seen immediately. We may choose to rebel against God and not see the negative effects immediately. Some people sow seeds of evil and destruction for years, and they think they have escaped God's judgment. But a time will come when those seeds take root. One day they will reap the harvest—in this life and in the life to come. One thing is certain: Disobedience, if allowed to continue, will result in death.

On the other hand, those who sow good seeds, through the Spirit of Christ, will reap a different harvest, one of love, faith, peace, and righteousness. It may also take time to see those results.

Paul knew this and admonished the Galatians not to grow weary: "Let us not become weary in doing good, for at the proper time we will reap a harvest, if we do not give up. Therefore, as we have opportunity, let us do good to all people, especially to those who belong to the family of believers" (Galatians 6:9-10). We must be patient and continue to sow good seeds. We inherit the promises of God through faith and patience, as Hebrews 6:12 states. But the spiritual laws we choose to walk in will affect our lives; depend on it!

Spiritual laws also chart the course for the destiny of nations. A country can rebel against God, while people live in prosperity. And because they are prosperous, they believe the bad seeds sown will not come into fruition. They may sing "Happy Days are Here Again." Yet, if they continue down that path of sensuality and materialism, they will soon sing the blues!

A nation can rebel against God for a brief period of time, while reaping the good seeds sown by their forefathers. "We have escaped the judgment of God," they reason in their hearts. However, though it takes some time for spiritual laws to take effect, consequences will, indeed, occur.

For example, the economy of a nation can be linked to spiritual laws. A nation who honors God will prosper, and bad economic times often signal corrupt seeds of the past. The economic policies initiated by government leaders often take years to take effect, and some administrations and congressional leaders attempt to take credit for good policies set into motion by previous administrations. But the truth will always remain: Those who respect God's commandments will lead our nation to prosperity. Those who reject His teachings will lead our nation to hard times.

> "Righteousness exalts a nation, but sin is a disgrace to any people."
>
> —Proverbs 14:34

Most people believe the prosperity of a nation depends upon its economic policies alone. Yet history proves the prosperity of a nation is in direct relation to its moral condition. God gives the leaders of a nation ability to enact good laws and policies. If the people as a majority turn their backs on God, corrupt leaders will certainly rise to power. Therefore, if a nation experiences turmoil, you will find rebellion in its recent past.

Even though they repent and return to God, it will usually take time to see positive effects. So, we cannot look at the outward appearances of a country, but at the current moral decisions, to anticipate their future blessing or discipline. Although any nation may endure hard times as a result of *past* moral failures, it will soon move into prosperity if its current leaders continue to rule righteously, and if its people remain focused on the Lord.

We must also remember a nation's current leaders may *not* have caused present judgment. At the same time, those leaders may also *not* be responsible for the country's prosperity. It's clear, much depends on seeds sown in the past. We must continue as a nation to sow good seed and patiently wait for its harvest.

Jesus Explains the Intent of the Law

God instructed the ancient Hebrews in moral, or spiritual laws, and in ceremonial, or symbolic laws. He gave Moses detailed instructions on moral ethics, sacrifices, feasts, and observances. Some people claim all spiritual laws became null and void after the New Covenant. This line of reasoning asserts, since we are free from the Law of Moses, there will be few or no consequences for our sins. Yet this argument is contrary to the Scriptures.

If we *refuse* to enter into the New Covenant provided by Christ, we will face the curses of breaking the Law. And even if we *are* under the New Covenant, we cannot deliberately continue unrepentant in sin without facing its consequences. Granted, we no longer have to observe the ceremonial laws like offering sacrifices and observation of feasts. God gave many of the feasts, which Israel was instructed to observe, as occasions of joy and celebration. He wanted the Hebrews to take time from their work to celebrate and enjoy life. Much in the ceremonial laws symbolized the work of Jesus. When taught and observed, these ceremonies pointed to the Messiah.

In addition, we don't have the heavy burden to observe animal sacrifices today, as the ancient Hebrews were instructed to do. Reading about these laws is still beneficial, though we are free from doing them.

Spiritual laws do remain in effect today. Jesus made this totally clear: "Do not think that I have come to abolish the Law or the Prophets; I have not come to abolish them but to fulfill them. I tell you the truth, until heaven and earth disappear, not the smallest letter, not the least stroke of a pen, will by any means disappear from the Law until everything is accomplished. Anyone who breaks one of the least of these commandments and teaches others to do the same will be called least in the kingdom of heaven, but whoever practices and teaches these commands will be called great in the kingdom of heaven. For I tell you that unless your righteousness surpasses that of the Pharisees and the teachers of the law, you will certainly not enter the kingdom of heaven" (Matthew 5:17-20).

The Pharisees were obsessively careful to observe the laws. They even created laws God didn't give. Notice how Jesus asserts with boldness that our righteousness must exceed the righteousness of those religious leaders. But if the Pharisees were so careful to observe the Laws of Moses, how can we ever expect our righteousness to exceed theirs?

Jesus continues with a sober discourse: "You have heard that it was said to the people long ago, 'Do not murder, and anyone who murders will be subject to judgment.' But I tell you that anyone who is angry with his brother will be subject to judgment. Again, anyone who says to his brother, 'Raca,' is answerable to the Sanhedrin. But anyone who says, 'You fool!' will be in danger of the fire of hell" (Matthew 5:21-22).

A New Theology?

To the Pharisees, Jesus introduced a radical new theology. But in essence, Jesus did not introduce a new theology. He merely explained the intents and purposes of God, concerning the Law and why He was sent.

Jesus reminded the Pharisees of ancient laws which instruct us not to commit adultery. Jesus not only reinforced this law, but He revealed its intent. Refraining from adultery is not enough. Under the new covenant, we are not even to look upon a woman with lust in our heart.

Not only did Jesus continue moral laws for actions, but He also took them to a new, higher level. This level dealt with intents and motives. This is the law of love, and it's where the Pharisees fell short.

> Let no debt remain outstanding, except the continuing debt to love one another, for he who loves his fellowman has fulfilled the law. The commandments, "Do not commit adultery," "Do not murder," "Do not steal," "Do not covet," and whatever other commandment there may be, are summed up in this one rule: "Love your neighbor as yourself." Love does no harm to its neighbor. Therefore love is the fulfillment of the law.
> —Romans 13:8-10

The Apostle Paul had received a revelation of the higher law, what I call the law of love. The law of love takes morality to a whole new level. If we love, we will not want to steal from our neighbor. We will not want to kill, even if we've been a victim of injustice. If we love someone, we will not want to have an affair with his wife.

Most important, if we love God, we will not want to offend Him. Love has no malice for his neighbor. This explains why Jesus came not to abolish the law, but to fulfill. Love is fulfilling the law. Love not only obeys the Ten Commandments, but love takes the Law of Moses to a higher level.

It appears He made the law even harder to obey. In fact, Jesus made obeying the law impossible! How is there hope? Does Jesus expect us to never think any lustful thoughts or never make a mistake? Does He demand our perfection? After all, He commanded us to be perfect, even as our Father in heaven is perfect (Matthew 5:48). Did Jesus give us commandments He knew we couldn't keep?

The Greek word translated "perfect" means complete. Jesus doesn't expect us to live a flawless life with no mistakes. He experienced the curse of mankind first hand, as He lived here on the earth. He knows the temptations of the flesh. But He does want us to have a perfect heart; a heart willing to be humble and repent; a heart that loves the Lord God; a heart that pursues God; a heart that loves righteousness.

We become righteous when we repent of our sins and make Jesus Lord of our lives. Upon surrendering to Christ, His righteousness is imparted to us. Receiving Christ as Lord is only the beginning. The Holy Spirit helps us to become holy. Holy means set apart. God is holy. He is set apart from the rest of His creation. He is set apart in glory, perfection, honor, wisdom, and power. He wants His children to be set apart and separated from the rest of the world.

Once we receive the atoning work of Christ, we begin the process of sanctification. Sanctification changes our way of thinking. It involves obedience to God's commandments and to the Holy Spirit. It comes by renewing our minds in God's Word. Throughout the Bible, we are given instructions on what is holy and unholy; what is clean and unclean. Holiness leads to peace and prosperity. It allows us to see God, to fellowship with Him. It leads to eternal life. Holiness leads to completeness in Christ or spiritual maturity. We have a part to play in becoming complete in Christ, by submitting to the Holy Spirit's correction.

He desires that we continue to grow spiritually, into a state of fullness, usefulness, fruitfulness, goodness, and holiness, into His very image. Jesus said in Luke 6:40 everyone who is fully trained would be like his teacher. No matter what great spiritual strides one has taken, or thinks they've taken, there's always room for improvement.

Nevertheless, it is possible to grow into spiritual maturity, so our faults are minimum rather than constant. By faith, we can grow in knowledge of Christ; sin can be an exception rather than common; good works can be as natural as breathing. But these things can only be done through Christ.

Jesus wanted to open the eyes of the Pharisees and the people. The Pharisees were full of pride and self-righteousness; they thought they obeyed all God's commandments. So Jesus revealed to us exactly how far we are from God's perfection. He showed the Pharisees how far they were from meeting God's requirements. "All mankind has sinned and fallen short of the glory of God," we read in Romans 3:23.

Jesus tried to lead everyone to godly sorrow, a broken and contrite spirit. He showed them their need for repentance, how much they needed a Savior. Yet, the Pharisees refused to admit they had not fully obeyed God's commandments. Because of pride, they could not see.

"If you were blind, you would not be guilty of sin; but now that you claim you can see, your guilt remains," Jesus said in John 9:41. He wanted the Pharisees to realize it was impossible for them to keep the law in their own strength or ability. God's law is directed at more than outward appearances. It addresses inward thoughts and intentions.

The Pharisees were deceived; they believed they were right with God, but were actually under the law's curse. They had fallen short and were headed for destruction, like any heathen or Gentile. Our own efforts of righteousness are filthy in the sight of God.

Christ came to redeem us from the law's curse. But only when we see our wretched condition do we realize we need a Savior. Christ redeemed us from the curse of the law by becoming a curse for us, for it is written: "Cursed is everyone who is hung on a tree." He redeemed us in order that the blessing given to Abraham might come to the Gentiles through Christ Jesus, so that by faith we might receive the promise of the Spirit, says Galatians 3:13-14.

Since believers are redeemed from the law's curse, does this mean we can continue to violate our conscience? If mighty men of God failed their attempts to obey the Law of Moses, how can we ever obey the higher law of Jesus today? After all, it is impossible to obey the higher law of love—or is it? The answer lies in our *new* covenant, made possible by Christ's blood.

> "This is the covenant I will make with the house of Israel after that time," declares the LORD. "I will put my law in their minds and write it on their hearts. I will be their God, and they will be my people."
>
> —Jeremiah 31:33

This is wonderful news! Through Jesus Christ we can have God's word written in our minds and hearts. We can know what is right or wrong for any situation we may face! Jesus sent the Holy Spirit to help us live righteous lives. And we overcome the sin in our lives by faith in the Holy Spirit's power within us. So redemption not only includes release from the curse of the law, but receiving the power—from God—to obey the law.

This power is included in the law of the Spirit of life. If we abide in Christ, we have the Holy Spirit's help, and we soon can find ourselves obeying more of God's commandments. Equally important, we are not burdened with a heavy yoke, trying to obey in our own human strength, because His Spirit—in us—changes our desires. It becomes a joy to obey. But it all starts with repentance, or a *willingness* to change.

If we *want* to obey God's commandments, *He will* help us do it! We aren't alone. If we sin, we can admit our sin and be cleansed from unrighteousness. We *can be* forgiven, because of the blood of the Lamb. So the Apostle Paul triumphantly declares in Romans 6:14: "For sin shall not be your master, because you are not under law, but under grace." We are not under the heavy burden of obeying the law with our own will power, but we are given the grace of God's Spirit, which grants us forgiveness and enables us to obey the moral laws. This is redemption's wonderful work, the Law of the Spirit of life.

Another reason why God brings judgment is to protect those with whom He has a covenant. The best known example is Noah, whom most of us know. God destroyed the corrupt generations in Noah's day by a flood to protect His covenant people. Only a few faithful were spared. But because of evil, God destroyed all other inhabitants on the earth.

Perhaps if God had not destroyed this vile generation, Noah and his family may have suffered bodily harm from the violent people on the earth. Even if they were not harmed physically, evil people might have corrupted Noah's family, leaving no righteous person on earth to be God's covenant partner. Let's look at other examples when God protected His covenant people:

Sodom and Gomorrah Judged

Abraham had a covenant with God because of faith. "Abraham believed God, and it was counted unto him as righteousness," says Romans 4:3. Lot also had a covenant with God, because he believed Abraham. When Abraham heard from God, Lot believed also, left his family, and followed. For Lot, this act of faith was counted as righteousness.

Later, because of obedience, both Abraham and Lot prospered, until there was not enough room for all their herds together. Consequently, strife arose between Abraham's servants and Lot's herdsmen. Eventually, they were forced to separate. Lot chose the greener pastures toward Sodom and Gomorrah. In the future, this unwise choice had a cost for Lot and his family. We soon find them living among the corrupt people in Sodom.

God allowed Sodom and Gomorrah to be captured by foreign kings. This served as a warning for them to turn from their evil ways. Since Lot chose to live in Sodom, he and his family were captured as well. When Abraham heard of the tragedy, he immediately set out to free them. God helped Abraham, and they routed the enemy. God destroyed the foreign kings, while He spared Sodom.

Since Lot believed Abraham was a man of God, God considered Lot a part of His covenant also. So it was because of Abraham, God's covenant friend, that Sodom was spared. Later, we see Lot still lives in decadent Sodom and Gomorrah, when the Lord appeared to Abraham, who was God's friend. God ate with Abraham and fellowshipped with him.

> When the men got up to leave, they looked down toward Sodom, and Abraham walked along with them to see them on their way. Then the LORD said, "Shall I hide from Abraham what I am about to do? Abraham will surely become a great and powerful nation, and all nations on earth will be blessed through him. For I have chosen him, so that he will direct his children and his household after him to keep the way of the LORD by doing what is right and just, so that the LORD will bring about for Abraham what he has promised him." Then the LORD said, "The outcry against Sodom and Gomorrah is so great and their sin so grievous that I will go down and see if what they have done is as bad as the outcry that has reached me. If not, I will know."
> —Genesis 18:16-21

God heard cries of the oppressed in Sodom and Gomorrah, like he heard Noah's cries in his evil generation. How can we act wickedly and think God doesn't know? When God's people live among violence and immorality, a cry goes out from their heart. Noah felt grieved by the rebellion around him. Likewise, degenerate people in Sodom and Gomorrah grieved Lot. A cry went up from those under God's covenant, and God heard their cry.

> For if God did not spare angels when they sinned, but sent them to hell, putting them into gloomy dungeons to be held for judgment. If he did not spare the ancient world when he brought the flood on its ungodly people, but protected Noah, a preacher of righteousness, and seven others. If he condemned the cities of Sodom and Gomorrah by burning them to ashes, and made them an example of what is going to happen to the ungodly. And if he rescued Lot, a righteous man, who was distressed by the filthy lives of lawless men, for that righteous man, living among them day after day, was tormented in his righteous soul by the lawless deeds he saw and heard. If this is so, then the Lord knows how to rescue godly men from trials and to hold the unrighteous for the Day of Judgment, while continuing their punishment.
> —II Peter 2:4-9

God destroyed Sodom and Gomorrah to protect Lot and his family from evil. According to the Apostle Peter, Lot felt vexed by the rampant corruption around him. Webster defines vexed as, "to bring trouble, distress, or agitation to, to bring physical distress, to irritate or annoy by petty provocations."[1]

A righteous man or woman will be and *should* be grieved by evil around us and in us. If we are not, something is wrong with our heart. If it does not irritate us when we see crimes, sex, violence, and other immorality on the evening news, then our conscience has become hardened. If it does not bother us to hear God's name used as a curse, then we have lost our fear and reverence for God. We must rend our hearts and come to Him for forgiveness and mercy. Lot did not allow his conscience to harden. He felt vexed by degeneracy; it is good he did.

I've wondered why Lot didn't take his family and leave earlier, if he was so grieved by the irreverent people in Sodom. Perhaps he was too comfortable. He probably had a nice house and plenty of interesting activities. Maybe it was too much trouble to uproot his family and move to the desert or mountains. Also, Lot probably realized his wife and sons-in-law had no desire to leave.

Whatever the reasons, it took angels of the Lord to rescue Lot and his family. Even then, his sons-in-law refused to leave, and his wife turned again toward home—to her great detriment. Abraham interceded on behalf of Sodom and Gomorrah because his nephew Lot lived there.

But God could not find ten righteous men, so the decision for total annihilation remained. God had to protect Abraham and Lot because of his covenant, his promise, but judgment had to come upon Sodom and Gomorrah.

Judgment of the Egyptians

In the story of Moses, we see another example of God's judgment to protect His covenant people. The Hebrew children were slaves in Egypt, enduring much hardship, injustice, and suffering. As with Noah and Lot, their cries went up to God. He could not ignore them, because they were His covenant people. So God sent a deliverer named Moses.

God commanded the Egyptian Pharaoh, "Let my people go." But Pharaoh's pride caused him to stubbornly refuse, told in Exodus 9:16. As a result, God sent judgments to warn Pharaoh and his Egyptian people. God will always give us plenty of time to repent before judgment comes. He is not willing that any should die.

He allowed His covenant people to remain slaves for four hundred years because He didn't *want* the Egyptians to perish. God sent frogs, hail, and many other signs to warn Pharaoh and his people. Likewise, He will send us signs, warning us of what lies ahead if we continue down a path of rebellion. But the Egyptians still refused to repent and believe. Finally, God sent the Angel of Death to destroy every first-born in Egypt, and Pharaoh's pride finally broke enough to let God's people leave.

But Pharaoh's pride asserted itself again and he regretted allowing the Israelites to depart from Egypt. God hardened his heart to glorify His name, explained in Exodus 14:4 and Romans 9:17. In an angry rage, Pharaoh took his army and pursued the Hebrews. No doubt he intended to slaughter many Hebrews and take the rest back to Egypt as slaves again.

This rebellion left God no choice but to destroy Pharaoh and his army. God was obligated to protect the Hebrews, since the Messiah was prophesied to come through His covenant people. God had already made a promise to Abraham that his seed would be as the stars in the heavens, and God's promises never fail.

God pronounces judgment to save the righteous, those with whom He has a covenant. So we see God destroyed the earth by a flood to spare Noah from wickedness. He destroyed Sodom for the sake of Abraham and Lot. In 2 Peter 2:7 we learn Lot felt continually vexed by Sodom's evil rebellion. Then God destroyed Pharaoh and his Egyptian army for the sake of His servant Moses and for the descendants of Abraham.

Did God love Noah more than the rest of his generation? Did God love Lot more than any in Sodom? Did God love the Egyptians any less than Moses and the Hebrews? No. All these righteous men had made a covenant with God. Then what separated the righteous from the wicked?

It's clear righteous people had a heart for God. They loved His fellowship. These faithful men and women believed God. They listened to His voice and by faith obeyed. They had a deep reverence and respect for the Almighty. They loved what God loved, hated what God hated, which should also be our goals. These men and women received grace in the eyes of the Lord. God gave His promise to protect them, and He was faithful.

Contrast that with evil men of the same generations. They heard God's voice through Noah, Abraham, Lot, and Moses. Yet, they loved evil more than God. Their hearts were prideful, bent toward evil, and they did not want God or what He represented. They refused to believe Noah, Lot, and Moses. They did not want God telling them what to do. Yet, even when destruction came, God still loved them.

If they had repented and changed their thinking, God would have spared them from their awful destruction. God gave them many years, hoping they'd listen and repent. However, they did not repent. And for the sake of the righteous, these evil men had to be destroyed.

Perfect and Just

A third reason God pronounces judgment is because He is holy and cannot coexist with evil. God is perfect and just; therefore, injustice must be punished. He knows evil will destroy peoples' lives. His justice also requires He step in to recompense those mistreated. When it comes to sin and death, God does condone hate—in the proper circumstance. God loves people, but He hates evil and all it represents.

Although God is love, He gets angry over injustice, sin, and rebellion. Transgression, iniquity, sickness, and death are all contrary to His nature. However, God's anger is controlled. And if we are born again by the blood of the Lamb, we have taken on God's personal nature. So, although we love people, we also hate evil and all it represents.

"Who gives you the right to tell us what is right and wrong?" is a question we hear. It amazes me when believers are accused of acting self-righteous. Some say we are intolerant because we believe Jesus when he said He is the *only* way of salvation. They say we are narrow-minded because we believe in right and wrong, good and evil, black and white. Others say Christians are judgmental when we simply accept and believe what God's Word says.

But the Bible is the inspired Word of the only living God. People may accuse us of cramming religion down their throats. But what they are really thinking in their hearts is, *I love evil. Let me do evil if I choose. Don't tell me or force me to do good. I want to be free to do evil around you, but don't you do good around me.* Because they have not been born from above, they are of their father, the devil. Light cannot coexist with darkness.

> Do not be yoked together with unbelievers. For what do righteousness and wickedness have in common? Or what fellowship can light have with darkness?
> —2 Corinthians 6:14

Paul does not admonish us to hate nonbelievers or mistreat the wicked, but to avoid close fellowship with them. We are not to shun them. At the same time, we are not to allow ourselves to become intimate with them.

Yes, Jesus was a friend of sinners, but not an intimate friend with them. He befriended them only from concern for their souls, as in Matthew 9:10-13. He didn't participate in their evil deeds. Like a little girl might be repulsed at seeing a snake, our nature should be disgusted at the sight of evil! As ambassadors for Christ, we must remember what Paul wrote in Ephesians 6:12: "We do not fight against flesh and blood, but against principalities and spiritual wickedness."

Jesus also instructed us in Matthew 5:44 to love those who may persecute us and do good to those who accuse us. People may be blinded with scales of darkness on their eyes and cannot see the truth. They often don't realize or understand what they do. This is why Jesus asked God to forgive the men who crucified Him. Though the wicked may reject him, Christ also bore their sins on a cross. He loves them, even as they are judged.

We can confront those who try to force their wicked ideas on us, while at the same time loving them. Love is the very reason we oppose them. We confront wicked acts and ideas and hope their eyes will open to the truth. Therefore, we can stand for uncompromising righteousness while at the same time extend a hand of mercy, much like a parent loves and disciplines a child.

Many who oppose truth believe they merely oppose a right-wing political conspiracy. Most who oppose biblical truth meditate little in God's Word. Oh yes, they may attend their local church faithfully, but it might only teach the traditions and opinions of men. But the next time someone tries to argue with you concerning abortion, gay rights, and other moral issues, ask them how often they read their Bible. Some people see issues only in a political sense, when the truth is these ideas are clearly addressed in the Bible.

God does not call homosexuality an inherited gene. He does not refer to adultery as an affair. Nowhere in the Bible does He describe infant murder as a free choice. Such immoral acts are an abomination to God. He still loves the people who do them, but He hates what they do. He not only hates their acts, but their actions make Him angry, because sin leads to death.

Yes, God gets angry. But it is a righteous, controlled anger. We can rest assured; those who continue to do evil *will* be judged. Maybe not in this life, but in the life to come.

When our Messiah returns to rule, His form of government will *not* be a democracy, but a theocracy. Whatever He speaks will occur. But because God is love, He will always give us free choice to obey or disobey. If we choose to obey, we will live with Him in His kingdom.

Those who choose to rebel will be cast out of His kingdom into outer darkness, separated forever from God. He must cast them out to protect those who believe and obey from being destroyed. His decisions will not be put to our vote. No protests will be tolerated, and we'll not dare to accuse the Holy One of unfairness.

We need to remember God is love, and each of God's acts are motivated by love. There are three simple truths. First, God is good and men, apart from Him, are evil. Next, contrary to the belief of some, God is also smarter than men. And finally, He is always right, never wrong.

If He was wrong even once, then He would not be God. So, those who are born of His Spirit will embrace His righteous government with joy. Those who love darkness will reject His love.

During the 1960s Charismatic movement, a revival of freedom swept the Church, encompassing all denominations. Like a breath of fresh air, this movement pumped new life into many suffocating bodies of believers. It sparked renewal everywhere.

The Jesus Movement among our youth spun-off from this Charismatic era. Many young people of the hippie generation found a personal relationship with Jesus. Many discovered Jesus to be a "really cool dude," a friend who sticks closer than a brother. It was a powerful movement of God.

Unfortunately, somewhere down the line we seem to have lost a holy fear and respect God deserves. It's true; believers have power to become the sons of God. Yet, we are not equal with God. Although we are adopted sons by the shed blood of Christ, we are still not equal with Christ.

One day every knee will bow to Jesus, not to His believers. Every tongue will confess that Jesus Christ is Lord, not His saints. We have His Holy Spirit within us, but without God we are only "dust in the wind." God is far above what we can even imagine or think. The Holy Spirit can only give us limited revelation, because our human flesh could not live if He revealed His glory in its fullness.

With this in mind, we know God is wiser than the wisest man. Even men like Solomon and Daniel were no comparison to the God of wisdom. This truth now established, why do men of our generation think of their ways as superior to God's? Why do the ungodly consider those who believe His Word simple and narrow-minded? Why are old-fashioned values despised as outdated relics of the past?

Considering themselves wise, our generation has become foolish, as Romans 1:22 says. This may be a revelation to some, but God is wiser than men. God has declared sin bad and righteousness good. There's no ambiguity in this matter. Evil is bad and righteousness is good. Sin brings destruction, righteousness results in prosperity. It *is* black and white.

God Hates Sin

God loves a sinner but hates the sin. Accordingly, we as disciples of Christ are commanded to love people, even to love our enemies, but hate their sin. God loves us, even when we live sinfully. However, God still hates sin.

Moreover, without repentance and the cleansing blood of Jesus, we can have no fellowship with God. We cannot try to clean up our lives with our own natural resolve, but we can come to Jesus as we are, with all our sins and bad habits. We must admit disobedience in our lives and a need for God's help. Then we receive His forgiveness and atonement by faith. Other religions have other forms of godliness. However, the Bible says in Hebrews 9:22, without the shedding of blood, there is no removal of sin.

When we surrender our will to His will and trust Him in every area of our lives, then we stand still and watch His work in us begin. God's Word, not man's opinion, is the standard we are to use to judge. When pastors and godly men call for our nation to repent and turn to righteousness, those who resist them are resisting God's Word. It is what we should live and die by. It leads us to eternal life. The world will pass away and all its lusts, but God's Word will stand forever.

Heaven and earth will pass away, but my words will never pass away.

—Matthew 24:35

God tells us He delights in justice, abhors all types of evil, and humbles prideful ones:

> This is what the LORD says: "Let not the wise man boast of his wisdom or the strong man boast of his strength or the rich man boast of his riches, but let him who boasts boast about this: that he understands and knows me, that I am the LORD, who exercises kindness, justice and righteousness on earth, for in these I delight," declares the LORD.
> —Jeremiah 9:23-24

God hates to see the poor and weak taken advantage of; as a matter of fact, it makes Him angry! He delights in showing kindness to those with a humble and contrite spirit. But judgment falls upon individuals and nations when they fail to understand and know God. We come to know Him when we spend time together and observe His ways, like any relationship. We understand Him by studying His Word, his letters to man.

Some people think God only delights in showing us kindness. While it's true God loves to be generous, to pour out His kindness to the humble in heart, at the same time, He also delights in justice and righteousness. God's justice entails judgment. God has emotions, along with self-control. He is long suffering, but He can also get angry, which the Bible refers to as "the cup of God's wrath" (Revelation 14:10).

God expects our reverence. Our Creator is not a tyrant who forces us to submit, but a loving Father who demands respect for providing our well-being. If we do not fear and respect Him, then we do not obey Him. Our failure to obey eventually results in our demise. But there will come a time when all creation will honor Him, even Satan and the fallen angels, as Romans 14:11 and Philippians 2:9-11 show us.

Because God is holy and cannot look upon sin, He will withdraw His presence from a person or nation who continually sins, with no desire to change.

> On that day I will become angry with them and forsake them; I will hide my face from them, and they will be destroyed. Many disasters and difficulties will come upon them, and on that day they will ask, "Have not these disasters come upon us because our God is not with us?"
> —Deuteronomy 31:17

When God withdraws His presence, all that He is departs from us. This includes His love, wisdom, peace, joy, guidance, and divine protection.

We can experience anguished separation and feel hopeless, all from rejecting God's commandments and choosing our own way. When God withdraws His holy presence from us, Satan comes in to kill, steal, and destroy. The Bible describes Hell as eternal separation from God. What is more tragic than separation from God now or later? Better to have never existed than to end up in such a wretched state.

God's Love

Because God is love, it leads to the final reason why He pronounces judgments. If Jesus did only good acts during His time on earth, how could He pronounce judgment? As we shall see, God's judgment is an act of love, which makes it also good.

Although we anger God with our rebellion, His motives are always from love. This important revelation is worth repeating again: "God's judgment is an act of love!" His actions are always born of love, which never forces its will on anyone. Otherwise, it wouldn't be love.

God gives all creation the freedom of choice, and some choose disobedience. Nevertheless, His love allows them that freedom, even if it leads to their own destruction. And those choices may not only destroy them, but the righteous as well. So, God would not act in love if He allowed evil to continue, which could eventually destroy His entire creation. God would be evil if He refused to do anything, so His law of justice has to be met. His solution was to give the ultimate sacrifice to save man.

> For God so loved the world that he gave his one and only Son, that whoever believes in him shall not perish but have eternal life.
> —John 3:16

Did God judge His only Son from anger? Absolutely not! God's goal saved mankind, but still, He left us with the power of choice. If we reject His Holy Son's sacrifice and follow evil, then God, by His very nature, must render judgment.

We realize that God allows judgment to bring us to surrender, because judgment *always* points to the Savior. It opens our eyes to His omniscience, omnipresence, and power. Judgment shows us we fall short of the perfection God requires, so it can save us from eternal death.

It's clear God thinks from a different perspective than man, who sees mostly the temporary, while God sees the eternal. Most people never see beyond their temporal needs in life. Granted, physical needs are necessary, but there is more to what we were created for than going to work, eating, sleeping, purchasing a home, buying a car, and entertainment.

Man tends to focus on what simply benefits his flesh, his five natural senses: taste, sight, touch, smell, and hearing. But God focuses on what builds man's spirit: love, joy, peace, faithfulness, gentleness, kindness, and patience are a few. We can obtain all these blessings when we obey the spiritual laws that God ordained before the universe.

Man was created a spirit being in a physical body that will die and decay, but his spirit will live forever! Everything in our physical realm is temporary, subject to change. But the spiritual realm will last forever, because God's word is spiritual; it too will stand forever!

Whatever we do in obedience to God will also last forever. This is why Jesus told His disciples to seek God's kingdom first, in Matthew 6:33. We are to make God's priorities ours. Our highest priority is to make our lives count for God's glory. Jesus told His disciples to seek righteousness above all things. Let's look at examples of God's priorities.

Sports are extremely popular in this generation. Most see sports as merely entertainment, competition, or a way to exercise. But how does God view sports? He has no problem with us enjoying them; however, His perspective differs from ours.

Man's highest priority is to win. Winning is somewhat important, but God emphasizes honesty, perseverance, courage, and fairness over a super bowl win or gold medal at any cost. These godly qualities make one a winner no matter what the score.

What about God's priorities about prosperity? He'd rather we live in peace than to allow riches to damn our souls. He'd rather we be generous to the poor than horde our riches. He'd choose sowing wisely for His kingdom over a self-centered, extravagant lifestyle. God says in Proverbs 21:20 He prefers prudence with wealth over wasting it on perishable things.

What does God think about famous people? Fame is not necessarily evil in itself. Many godly people have become famous, including Jesus Himself. However, Proverbs 29:25 and Ezekiel 16:14-15 imply that obedience is better than compromise with men to obtain fame. Fame should not be one's driving ambition, says James 3:14-15. And Matthew 6:33 instructs us to seek righteousness above all things.

God's perspective on how we live this short life is much different than men's perspective. To shine forth righteousness and make a difference is more commendable to God than to live comfortable lives, says Matthew 16:24-27. Eternity's rewards far exceed the temporary rewards of this life, says Matthew earlier in 6:1-6, 16-21. And He teaches us honor from God greatly outweighs honor from men in Matthew 5:11-12.

We must consecrate ourselves to do God's will, even if it means hardship and suffering. We need to practice keeping our eyes on eternal rewards, looking to Jesus, the author and finisher of our faith, then we can learn to see all things from God's perspective.

In his best-selling book, *The Purpose Driven Life*, Rick Warren makes this wise observation, "What happens outwardly in our life is not as important as what happens inside us. Circumstances are temporary, but our character lasts forever."[2]

We can tell by this statement that Rick Warren can see from God's perspective. Let me take it upon myself to further clarify this statement by Pastor Warren. God would rather we go through suffering while living in obedience and holiness, than to have riches and be slaves to sin. God loves us so much that He allows us to suffer to keep us on the path of truth.

Of course, His perfect will is for us to walk in truth and live in prosperity. Nevertheless, if we stubbornly rebel, God has no alternative but to discipline. That's the essential truth of this entire book: God's judgment and discipline is an act of mercy!

Man sees judgment as an angry, cruel reaction to what we do. But this is only the blind, logical thinking of man. God's judgment is an act of love.

> It was good for me to be afflicted so that I might learn your decrees.
> —Psalm 119:71

I know, O LORD that your laws are righteous, and in faithfulness you have afflicted me.
—Psalm 119:75

The psalmist was persecuted because he loved God's law. In verse 69 he says, "The arrogant have smeared me with lies." Yet because of these afflictions, the psalmist returned to the Lord. He turned to God for help and comfort. As a result, he studied God's statutes even more diligently. And the more he studied, the more he learned.

Stay on God's Side

We cannot comprehend God's ways unless the Holy Spirit reveals them to us. But even when we don't understand, we must continue to trust Him anyway. We need to stay on God's side, because we know He is good!

Most of us have no idea of the destruction awaiting evil people. If we did, we'd make more of an effort to avoid sin. God knows the horrible damage evil inflicts on mankind. Like a cancer, sin can spread from generation to generation. And like a wildfire it spreads, leaving nothing but destruction and desolation behind.

God's judgment is like surgery; it removes a cancer and stops its relentless advance. God may use means that men may consider cruel to extinguish evil. Just as firemen employ more fire or an explosion to prevent further spread of a wildfire, God sometimes uses destruction of a few to prevent total annihilation of all mankind. His judgment may seem cruel, but it halts the spread of evil.

God's perfect will is for His people to pray in every situation. Prayer allows Him to work, even in the hearts of evil people in authority, to change their minds and bring about goodness. In addition, prayer allows God's angels to intervene, to avoid many situations of death and destruction. However, when people harden their hearts to the point where there is no chance for repentance, God may have no other choice than to use force to overcome evil.

The death penalty is a good example of judgment enacted to overcome evil. God instilled it through Noah, after the flood, as Genesis 9:6 shows. The death penalty sometimes prevents evil from spreading today, as it did after the great flood. God instituted it as a deterrent to evil, as Exodus 21:12 explains. Without punishment, there is less fear of judgment and no accountability, Proverbs 21:15 tells us. So, though it seems cruel, strong consequences are necessary to prevent violence from exploding throughout the earth.

If God had failed to enact the death penalty, it's possible another world-wide event of catastrophic proportion may have been necessary at some time. God reaffirmed the death penalty through Moses, centuries later, as Deuteronomy 19:13 shows.

Some people ask, "What if a person on death row accepts Christ. Shouldn't they be forgiven and released?" For one, we can't know what's truly in a person's heart. They may be sincere or say anything to avoid death. Only God and the person know for sure.

Second, even if they are sincere, the death penalty must still be carried out, because it serves as a deterrent for others who would do violence, explained in Deuteronomy 13:8-11; 17:12-13; 19:18-21; 21:21. So although the person is forgiven and clean in God's sight, as though they have never committed a crime, they must still adhere to the laws of the governing authority.

We may question, "Didn't Jesus abolish the death penalty when he commanded us to turn the other cheek?"

> You have heard that it was said, "Eye for eye, and tooth for tooth." But I tell you, do not resist an evil person. If someone strikes you on the right cheek, turn to him the other also.
> —Matthew 5:38-39

Jesus spoke here, not to government authorities, but to His disciples. He taught them how to react in love, if they suffer persecution for righteousness.

As Christ's disciples, we are not to seek personal revenge, but forgive and pray for our enemies. If we continue to love and pray for those who have wronged us, it will open their eyes to see the goodness of God, perhaps leading them to repentance.

We entrust ourselves to God, who will bring about revenge and justice through angels or through governing authorities. We are to avoid strife and seek peace when possible, like 1 Peter 3:11 shows us. However, Jesus never taught to avoid defending the helpless and innocent. God is a defender of the orphan and the widow, as Psalm 68:5 states.

At no time in His ministry do we see Jesus speak against Roman law. As long as they didn't contradict God's law, He respected and obeyed the governing authorities. Even when the thief who was dying on a cross next to Jesus repented and asked our Savior to remember him when He came into His kingdom, Jesus didn't release him from the death penalty. The King of Kings could have used his authority and sent legions of angels to rescue the repentant thief from the cross, as Matthew 26:53 shows. But He allowed the soldiers to carry out Roman law.

Christ left the death penalty intact, as decreed by God to Noah and Moses. He allowed the repentant thief to die beside Him that sacred day, even though the man received Christ as his Savior while dying on a cross. But Jesus gave him something better than salvation from pain and physical death. He promised eternal life.

> "We are punished justly, for we are getting what our deeds deserve. But this man has done nothing wrong." Then he said, "Jesus, remember me when you come into your kingdom." Jesus answered him; "I tell you the truth, today you will be with me in paradise."
>
> —Luke 23:41-43

The Savior was aware that many would reject Him as Lord and continue their murderous ways. Jesus realized that without the death penalty, lawlessness and violence would get out of control, perhaps endangering the entire human race.

Similarly, war can be good or bad, depending on its purpose. Mighty warrior Joshua was raised by God to destroy evil and give the Promised Land to Israel. Then and today, believer's prayers are the best weapons for warfare. However, when God's people fail to persevere in prayer, God may use war to end specific evil powers. When a nation goes to war to stop the cruel tyranny of another nation, it is a noble cause. When a nation goes to war to set the oppressed free, it is a worthy sacrifice.

For example, God instructed Joshua and his army to destroy entire villages and nations. In a few instances, nations were so evil that God didn't want any person or animal left alive. He didn't want evil to spread among Israel, thereby defiling them.

Today we live under a better covenant. We have Jesus Christ's power to halt evil's spread. Thankfully, the Gospel's power can change any person, no matter how deep the darkness in their lives. Nevertheless, God still uses war to overcome evil.

Some peace advocates claim that Jesus preached against war. Therefore, they declare we must resist war at all costs. Jesus did preach against hatred, violence, and taking revenge into our own hands. We, *as individual* believers, should never initiate violence, if at all possible. We are children of peace. No matter how much evil is done to us, we are to continue to love our enemies, as Jesus commanded.

However, this doesn't mean we should protest against honorable governments and authorities who try to defend nations from evil tyranny. Jesus and the early apostles never preached against the Roman government or its military. As a matter of fact, the only New Testament scriptures on government authorities involve admonitions for us to submit to them. This implies the military and police who enforce the governments' authority, as well.

At one point in the Scriptures, Jesus told his disciples that whoever doesn't have a sword, sell his robe and buy one, in Luke 22:36. If we interpret this scripture in its context, Jesus wasn't advocating that His disciples take up arms against the Jewish authorities or the Roman government. Rather, He was attempting to help His disciples see the gravity of the situation at hand. In just a matter of hours, He would stand trial before the Jewish leaders. He knew His followers would not fight, but run in fear, forsaking Him, leaving Him to die alone on the cross. This was His purpose for coming to earth.

Yet, we can infer from this statement that there may be times when we as Christians are called upon to help government authorities bring justice; to protect the innocent, helpless, orphans, and widows; to help overthrow evil tyranny, even using force if necessary. A Christian's most effective weapons are prayer and persuasive speaking.

There is little doubt that God hates war's destruction, mentioned in Isaiah 2:4. God is love, but also can be the God of war, especially when He brings judgment to His creation, as in Isaiah 13:4-5. Indeed, the Old and New Testament scriptures indicate there are times when God will lead believers into war, to stem the tide of evil and usher in peace. Joel 2:1-11 and Revelation 19:11-21 speak of this.

So we should definitely esteem our military and policemen with honor. There are always people who declare all militaries are evil, yet they have no problem with policemen, who protect us from murderers and thieves. They even express gratitude toward police and hold them in high esteem for their protection from lawlessness—as well they should! Yet, these same individuals seem to consider our military evil, which protects us from lawlessness on a worldwide scale.

The Nazis claimed to be Christians, yet they were totally deceived. They annihilated anyone whom, in their opinion, slowed the progress of their superior race. Pride prevented them from seeing the truth. So God had no choice but to send Australian, British and American forces to stem their tide of evil. World War II was ugly and cruel, but steps had to be taken to douse the fires of fascism.

A more recent historical situation of terrorism in the 21st Century is a good analogy. Terrorism results from a cancer of hatred. And like the Nazis, Muslim extremists believe they have a God-ordained right to spread their hatred around the world. They are too prideful to see any possibility of being wrong. Then once again, God sent British and American forces to put out the literal flames of terrorism.

Dissidents marched and protested the war. They never considered the alternative. Terrorism could spread worldwide, including into their peaceful, free neighborhoods. The result would be a world ruled by intimidation and fear.

Again, God moved upon the leaders of the United States, Great Britain, and other nations to extinguish the fires of terrorism. As a result, the ones who protested the Middle East war are free from inevitable intimidation and fear of terrorist control. Thanks to those who courageously stood for preservation of life and liberty, the world has a better chance to live in peace. War is cruel. But in many cases, the alternative is worse.

Our Christian Church experienced a spiritual regression in the 1990s. This lapse of zeal allowed terrorism to build a stronghold and resulted in destruction of thousands of American lives and millions of dollars in property on September 11, 2001. But when God's people begin to earnestly pray for Arab nations, as they did for Eastern Europe during the Cold War, their religious oppression will fall, as the Iron Curtain fell. Prayer can destroy spiritual strongholds of terrorism in any century, without a shot fired.

God will always find a way to destroy evil so goodness, mercy, and truth can prevail. Jesus knew the destructive force of evil, and He wanted us to know the serious consequences of sin.

> You have heard that it was said, "Do not commit adultery." But I tell you that anyone who looks at a woman lustfully has already committed adultery with her in his heart. If your right eye causes you to sin, gouge it out and throw it away. It is better for you to lose one part of your body than for your whole body to be thrown into hell. And if your right hand causes you to sin, cut it off and throw it away. It is better for you to lose one part of your body than for your whole body to go into hell.
> —Matthew 5:27-30

Most people consider the drastic consequences in these verses might prevent a man from lusting for a woman. Granted, Jesus probably didn't intend we immediately pluck out our eyes. He expects us to repent before it comes to the point of self mutilation by removal of a hand or an eye. But Jesus meant what He said: It is better to maim yourself than to go to hell.

Thank goodness Jesus Christ's power provides forgiveness and helps us resist sins. Because of His sacrifice, we don't have to resort to drastic measures of self control or self discipline. People often overlook these scriptures, reasoning, *Since God is love, He wouldn't do such a thing.*

Yes, God is love. However, in contrast, they err to believe there is no hell, and He never brings destruction. But He does judge—because He is love! It may seem cruel in man's natural understanding, but His judgment is often a final warning, to keep us from eternal death. God's discipline influences men to repent, and His kindness may also bring many to repentance. Nevertheless, some hearts become so hard, only the fear of judgment pushes them to repent.

> Be merciful to those who doubt; snatch others from the fire and save them; to others show mercy, mixed with fear—hating even the clothing stained by corrupted flesh.
> —Jude, verse 22-23

The King James translation says, "...others, save with fear." God's judgment might be necessary to pull men from hell's fire. But His motives are always from love. Judgment is a result of *our* choices. After judgment, He will always comfort us.

The good news is that God's judgments are avoidable. He will shower people and nations with kindness so they may see His goodness and desire to be like Him. He sent His prophets to Israel to give them the chance to repent. He also sent Jonah to warn Nineveh, enabling them to repent and avoid judgment. Finally, He sent His Son, Jesus, to give us a way of escape from eternal judgment. God is not willing that any should die, as the familiar verse John 3:16 says. However, the Bible says that God will not always strive with mankind. If we continue to reject His warnings and kindness, there will come a time of judgment.

Restoration follows judgment, as it is written in James 2:13: "Mercy triumphs over judgment." There are many other examples of this throughout the Scriptures. We see God's prophets warn of judgment—over and over. God gives people plenty of time to repent.

However, eventually there's a time when the cup of God's wrath is filled, and discipline is given. Even after judgment, He doesn't reject His people. We always find Him waiting, ready to receive all who repent and call on His name.

Contrary to erroneous interpretations of theology, God *does* get angry over sin and rebellion. Pride, unbelief, hypocrisy, injustice, and worshipping other things can anger God. He gets angry when we continually treat Him with irreverence and disrespect. But His anger is always controlled, because He is perfect self-control. And like a good parent, when He gets angry His consequences are motivated by love.

God brings judgment on individuals, His Church, on rulers, and on nations to induce peace. In the following chapters, we will look at His ways to deal with individuals and groups.

Fruit Inspection

1. List reasons why judgment comes:
   _____
   _____
   _____
   _____

2. Why do the righteous suffer?
   _____
   _____
   _____
   _____

3. Think of times you or others have suffered:
   _____
   _____
   _____
   _____

   Did you believe God worked on your behalf, despite the circumstances?
   _____
   _____
   _____

4. Why did God establish natural and spiritual laws?

   What happens when we break those laws?

5. When have you observed the law of sowing and reaping in your life or others?

6. Describe how this law of sowing and reaping affects:

   Nations–

   Governments–

Churches–

Schools–

Businesses–

Homes–

7. Did Jesus come to abolish the Law of Moses?

WHY GOD'S LOVE BRINGS JUDGMENT • 73

What laws did He fulfill, as in Matthew 5:17?
_____
_____
_____
_____

8. What law did Jesus establish when he came to earth, in John 13:34?
_____
_____
_____
_____

How does this law differ from the Law of Moses?
_____
_____
_____
_____

9. Why did God destroy Sodom and Gomorrah and spare Lot? Why does God protect some and destroy others?
_____
_____
_____
_____

10. Why couldn't Moses see God's face in Exodus 33:18-20?
_____
_____
_____
_____

11. How can we become holy?

Psalm 4:3–

John 17:17–

Ephesians 5:26–

Hebrews 13:12–

12. What are the benefits of holiness?
    Romans 6:22–

Hebrews 12:14–

3 John 1:2–

13. Why does God hate sin?

John 10:10–

Romans 5:12–

Romans 6:23–

Romans 7:5–

14. Does God get angry?

Psalm 38:1–

Psalm 76:7–

Mark 3:5–

Hebrews 4:3–

What motivates God's anger?

15. What is God's motive for judgment upon the earth, in 1 John 4:8 and Isaiah 40:5?

16. How are men's priorities different from God's?

What are the most important priorities of your life?

17. Why does God seem to use cruel means to destroy evil?

18. Is the death penalty ever necessary to destroy evil?

   Why or why not, from Deuteronomy 13:8-11?

19. Is war ever needed to destroy evil?

   Why or why not, in Joshua 6:21?

   Why or why not, in Revelation 19:11-21?

_____
_____

20. Some people consider Christ's cross a cruel way to destroy evil. Why was the death of God's Son a necessary evil, in John 3:16?

_____
_____
_____
_____

CHAPTER 3

JUDGING THE FRUIT OF RIGHTEOUSNESS

Until now, we have examined why God judges. We've established the premise that God brings judgment because He loves mankind. Now let's explore different spheres of society to which judgment comes. First, let's look at how God judges individuals, and how we can discern a person's fruit.

How does God judge an individual? Foremost, He judges a person based on whether or not one believes and receives Jesus Christ as Lord of his or her life, as in Acts 16:31. God also judges mankind according to their fruit or character. The term "bearing fruit" can mean souls we win to Christ, whether we influence others toward righteousness or evil, as well as good works and character.

God is Supreme Judge; He is wiser than men. He judges not by appearances, but by our hearts. When our Messiah returns to judge the nations, He will judge our motives also, not how we appear to live, as in Isaiah 11:3-4.

Have you ever been accused of an evil motive when your intention was actually good? I'm sure everyone has been falsely accused at some point in their life. But when God judges us someday, there will be no mistakes, no false accusations, no injustice, and no hypocrisy. He is faithful and true; He searches our hearts.

> I the LORD search the heart and examine the mind, to reward a man according to his conduct, according to what his deeds deserve.
> —Jeremiah 17:10

We, as mere men, cannot discern even our own hearts, much less the heart of someone else. For this reason, we must be slow to form an opinion of others. We must never jump to quick conclusions nor judge strictly by how things appear. We will never fully know the mind, motives, or heart of others, or even of ourselves, until the Day of Judgment, when God brings everything into the open for all to see.

> I care very little if I am judged by you or by any human court; indeed, I do not even judge myself. My conscience is clear, but that does not make me innocent. It is the Lord who judges me. Therefore judge nothing before the appointed time; wait till the Lord comes. He will bring to light what is hidden in darkness and will expose the motives of men's hearts. At that time each will receive his praise from God.
> —I Corinthians 4:3-5

We, as born again Christians, have a Greater One living in us. And while we cannot know fully what is in a person's heart, we can discern, to a certain extent, his beliefs. With the help of the Holy Spirit, we can discern a person's heart with remarkable accuracy, after taking plenty of time to weigh and observe the evidence. Of course, this is only a fraction of a person's thoughts. We won't ever know his every thought and intent as God does. Nevertheless, God's Spirit will enable us to discern enough to know whether a person is producing good or evil fruit.

Since God is the only one who knows what is in a person's heart, He is "The Great Fruit Inspector." We're not to go around looking for faults in others. However, Jesus instructed His disciples on how to discern or judge the fruit of others, to prevent them from being led astray and devoured by wolves in sheep's clothing. He cared for His sheep and taught them how to recognize deception. According to Jesus, those who have His indwelling Spirit should be able to discern the good and bad fruit of others in our daily interactions with them. If we're able to discern good and bad fruit, we won't be deceived.

A Tree and Its Fruit

As rulers with Christ, let's look at the correct approach to judging one's fruit. It's true we cannot search someone's heart like God, yet there are limited ways we can discern. One way is to observe their actions, whether they produce good or evil.

> Watch out for false prophets. They come to you in sheep's clothing, but inwardly they are ferocious wolves. By their fruit you will recognize them. Do people pick grapes from thorn bushes, or figs from thistles? Likewise every good tree bears good fruit, but a bad tree bears bad fruit. A good tree cannot bear bad fruit, and a bad tree cannot bear good fruit. Every tree that does not bear good fruit is cut down and thrown into the fire. Thus, by their fruit you will recognize them.
> —Matthew 7:15-20

We can discern what is in a person's heart by his fruit. With the help of the Spirit of Christ, it is relatively simple to discern his heart, because a good tree bears good fruit and a bad tree bears corrupt fruit. To understand the difference, we must be born again, with God's nature in us.

We must put to death our old nature, which was corrupted by the prince of darkness, and put on the nature of Christ. How do we do that? We renew our mind by spending time in the Word of God, while trusting in the Holy Spirit to reveal His truth.

To discern truth, we must also walk in love and humility. If we walk in love, we can judge with compassion. When we walk in humility, we are able to receive correction, resulting in discernment of the truth. Only when we act in love and humility can we become skilled in righteousness. It takes time spent with a person before we can discern his motives. When we take time to observe him and his fruit, we can really know that person.

Remember how Jesus cautioned us to beware of false prophets. He said they would come in sheep's clothing. Sometimes people may appear to have good fruit on the outside. They have a charismatic personality, smile, and seem to say the right things. They may have a striking appearance and elegant charm. But if you look beyond their outward appearance and look deeper into their hearts, into their motives, they are devious, ravenous wolves.

On the other hand, a person may lack charm and personality. He or she may have an ordinary or even sloppy appearance. He may not give a good first impression, but still have character, abilities, and perseverance to rise to greatness.

I think of Albert Einstein. He was not striking in appearance. On the surface, he seemed like an ordinary man who was somewhat eccentric. His clothing was unkempt. Sometimes he didn't even comb his hair. On occasion, he appeared in public with different-colored socks. He felt these things were trivial compared to the laws of physics; he took little time for them. After many years of strenuous, focused concentration, he became absent-minded.

A story about Albert Einstein traveling on a train relates that as a young conductor collected tickets, Einstein began to search everywhere for his boarding pass.

"Sir, you do not need to show me your ticket. I know who you are," the conductor said.

"You don't understand. I need to find out where I am going," Einstein replied.

This was one of the most brilliant men to walk the face of the planet. He discovered many laws of physics and how they operate. And the more he learned, the more he realized the vastness and complexity of our universe. In later years, he eventually found a deep respect for his Creator. Our world tends to promote those who look good in outward appearance. But we know God judges men from the heart.

> Charm is deceptive, and beauty is fleeting; but a woman who fears the LORD is to be praised.
> —Proverbs 31:30

When God instructed Samuel to appoint a king over Israel, Samuel thought it might surely be Jesse's eldest son, who apparently had a striking appearance. But God chose Jesse's youngest son David instead. God saw something in David's heart others couldn't see. These qualities later emerged, as the story unfolds. David was a man of faith and courage, and he produced good fruit. David is remembered in history as one of the greatest kings of all time. God saw this in David's character when he was still a young lad.

God sees what men cannot see. How can we know what is in a person's heart? The truth is we can't, unless the Spirit of God helps us. One way to discern the heart is by listening to a person's conversation.

> Make a tree good and its fruit will be good, or make a tree bad and its fruit will be bad, for a tree is recognized by its fruit. You brood of vipers, how can you who are evil say anything good? For out of the overflow of the heart the mouth speaks. The good

man brings good things out of the good stored up in him, and the evil man brings evil things out of the evil stored up in him. But I tell you that men will have to give account on the Day of Judgment for every careless word they have spoken. For by your words you will be acquitted, and by your words you will be condemned.
—Matthew 12:33-37

Many times there is an initial way I can tell much about a person after only a few minutes of conversation. How is that? By what comes out of his mouth! One whose mouth is filled with curses reveals that he lives under a curse, or he's developed some bad speaking habits which he needs to overcome.

The mouth of the righteous brings forth wisdom, but a perverse tongue will be cut out. The lips of the righteous know what is fitting, but the mouth of the wicked only what is perverse.
—Proverbs 10:31-32

Then there are those who constantly complain. Some slander and gossip about others. They lash out with tongues like swords, attempting to destroy another's reputation and self-esteem. They recklessly shoot words like piercing arrows, which cut to the heart. Other people's conversations are peppered with vulgar, perverse language.

The mouth of the righteous is a fountain of life, but violence overwhelms the mouth of the wicked.
—Proverbs 10:11

And many people always speak negative words of unbelief, which must please Satan, who is a negative being. Perhaps he has good reason. Since Satan rebelled and fought against the Creator, he has nothing to look forward to any longer. Adam yielded his authority and dominion to Satan when he disobeyed God. And because God refers to Satan as the prince of this world in John 12:31, those who allow themselves to be influenced by the world's systems tend to talk negatively. We can see how it doesn't take long to discern what is in a person's heart.

> A truthful witness gives honest testimony, but a false witness tells lies. Reckless words pierce like a sword, but the tongue of the wise brings healing.
> —Proverbs 12:17-18

We've seen how you can discern a person's likes and dislikes by his words. But we can also tell what emotions he is feeling. A person's speech reveals his feelings, as well as beliefs and values. There are those who never stop talking, and others who hardly say a word. It seems reasonable then; the one who speaks sparingly has less chance of sinning with his mouth.

> My dear brothers, take note of this: Everyone should be quick to listen, slow to speak and slow to become angry.
> —James 1:19

Have you ever been with a person who always seems to lift you up? After conversing you feel strengthened, peaceful, loved. These types of people usually have no shortage of friends. Words of kindness, words of wisdom, and words of life are what flow from the mouth of the righteous. Love is an attribute of the righteous, which is positive and always expects the best. Love encourages others and bears or shares their burdens. A loving, righteous person's mouth is a fountain of life and health, a blessing to themselves and all around them.

A second way to judge people is by observing what they do. John the Baptist spent much time addressing this issue among the people of Israel, at a time when many in Israel had learned the Torah since childhood. The Torah was the written laws of Moses and other laws. People were taught God's law but did not apply it in their lives. To them it was only tradition.

We can judge people by what they do. Are they doers of the Word or only hearers? Do they act like what they say? Do they go about doing good or evil? We'll be held accountable to God not only for what we say, but what we do, as well.

In some cases, we'll be judged for what we *don't* do. Do we feed the hungry? Do we visit those in prison? Do we show compassion to the weak and sick? Do we comfort those who mourn? Do we feed the Great Shepherd's lambs? Do we obey what the Holy Spirit is telling us to do?

Let's compare people to trees bearing fruit. First, we can know a person's heart by his words. A corrupt tree speaks corruption. A good tree speaks words of truth and life. Second, a good tree produces righteous actions that will automatically lead us to obey God's commands. A corrupt tree produces bad fruit. The Bible clearly states that those who continually produce corrupt fruit will not inherit the kingdom of God.

> But the fruit of the Spirit is love, joy, peace, patience, kindness, goodness, faithfulness, gentleness and self-control. Against such things there is no law.
> —Galatians 5:22-23

> The acts of the sinful nature are obvious: sexual immorality, impurity and debauchery; idolatry and witchcraft; hatred, discord, jealousy, fits of rage, selfish ambition, dissensions, factions and envy; drunkenness, orgies, and the like. I warn you, as I did before, that those who live like this will not inherit the kingdom of God.
> —Galatians 5:19-21

Purging to Yield More Fruit

We've looked at ways to discern a person's fruit. God has a sharper way of judging one's fruit. He can go directly to the mind and heart to discern our motives. He knows our hearts better than we ourselves. Sometimes we are deceived and don't even realize our misguided intentions. Many times we simply don't know what we think or do is wrong. If we ask, He will reveal our motives so we can change and become more like Jesus.

God not only judges our fruit, but He works in us so we can bear greater fruit. Once we begin to produce good fruit, He purges us so we can produce even more. Let's search the Scriptures to find how we can grow good fruit. In order to do so, we must be purged. There are two ways God does this.

> I am the true vine, and my Father is the gardener. He cuts off every branch in me that bears no fruit, while every branch that does bear fruit he prunes so that it will be even more fruitful.
> —John 15:1-2

First, He purges us by His Word; by it God searches our hearts. It reveals to us what is unclean. It examines our motives and divides right from wrong. God's Word may hurt our flesh, but in the end, will yield the peaceable fruit of righteousness.

> For the word of God is living and active. Sharper than any double-edged sword, it penetrates even to dividing soul and spirit, joints and marrow; it judges the thoughts and attitudes of the heart
> —Hebrews 4:12

God's Word, under the Holy Spirit's power, convicts us of sin. His Word shows areas of our lives which need change. Some people skip over this part of God's Word; they want only to hear about blessings. But we must receive all God's instructions, including correction and holiness—as well as blessings.

Many mistake the convicting power of the Holy Spirit for condemnation. God's conviction will lead us to repentance and life, because it provides a way out of sin through Jesus Christ, but condemnation only leads to death, with no way out. Conviction provides hope; condemnation is only hopelessness. Conviction leads to God consciousness; condemnation leads to sin consciousness.

Yet there are many who do not know the difference. Some claim they are Christian yet continue to practice sin, with no conviction acknowledged in their lives. When God tries to convict them of sin, they brush it off and think it is condemnation. When true servants of God attempt to confront them, they arrogantly defend a sinful lifestyle and accuse those whom God sent as self-righteous, intolerant, and judgmental.

However, the Holy Spirit will continue to convict us of our need to change. This does not lead to condemnation but freedom from the yoke of sin and death. There is no peace and joy for the wicked, as in Isaiah 48:22.

Second, God purges us by allowing trials, persecutions, and afflictions. It's appropriate to discuss this subject at length, because it is greatly misunderstood by many believers. But before we go further, let me make it perfectly clear I do *not* suggest God *wants* us sick or afflicted.

Jesus was God in the flesh. Never once is it recorded that He struck anyone with a sickness or plague. Acts 10:38 says, "Jesus went around doing good and healing all who were under the power of the devil." From this scripture, we know it is the devil who oppresses and afflicts. God heals, delivers, restores, and does good.

James 1:17 says, "Every good and perfect gift is from above, coming down from the Father of the heavenly lights, who does not change like shifting shadows." Sickness, like sin, is the devil's work, either directly or indirectly. It entered into the world with the curse, when man disobeyed God in the Garden of Eden.

This doesn't imply that everyone who is sick has some type of sin in his or her life. Sometimes a person's actions or words may have nothing to do with his becoming ill. Sickness can result from natural laws being set into motion due to the curse, as in John 9:3. No matter what the source of sickness is, God desires for His children to prosper.

> Beloved, I wish above all things that you may prosper and be in health, even as your soul prospers.
> —3 John 2

God wants us to live a peaceable life, serve Him, and produce much fruit. Like we want to see our children obey and prosper, God desires His best for us. For this reason, He sent His Son so that man could be forgiven and born again with God's nature.

Notice the apostle John also desired that the Church prosper, as the soul prospers. This statement unlocks a truth that is often overlooked by many believers. It is essential for our soul to prosper before we can walk in true prosperity. True prosperity is not only material blessings, but also includes a healthy body and mind. What good is material wealth if one has no peace or joy? God wants us to prosper, as a father does his son.

When God created man and placed him in the Garden of Eden, He never intended man to suffer. It hurts God to see His creation groaning in pain. Before the fall, there was no suffering for men or animals in Eden. When men live with God in the New Jerusalem, there will be no more suffering or death. God is not the source of sin, sickness, war, and death. Sin, sickness, and death come as a result of separation from God. Hell is a place of torment because it is a place totally separated from God. He is the source of life and all that pertains to life. Yet, after the fall of Adam and Eve, physical death became necessary if men were to ever have the chance to restore their relationship with God. Once the curse came upon mankind, he could no longer fellowship with God in his corrupted flesh. The death of God's Son was the only way to restore both spiritual and physical life to all those who would believe and receive Him.

Why Do Afflictions Come?

Having established this essential truth, why then do afflictions come? We have an enemy who loves to destroy us. Satan and his minions will always contend with the children of God! The enemy of our souls will attempt to inflict hardships and afflictions upon God's people. His purpose is to stop God's anointing. If we give him an opportunity, he will rush in like a roaring lion, as 1 Peter 5:8 says. Satan wants to damage the fruit in our lives.

If he can't destroy us with afflictions, he'll use comfort and ease to lull us into our demise. But comfort and ease is never the goal of Christ's true disciples. A believer's purpose on earth is to bear fruit—good fruit! Satan is obviously not concerned about Christians who are lulled to sleep in comfort; they are no threat. But he'll contend with those bearing fruit for God's kingdom. He will find a way to attack.

Sometimes afflictions come when God allows natural and spiritual laws—which he set up—to operate in our lives, without intervention. In essence, this is a indirect form of purging. We've discussed natural and spiritual laws at length in chapter 2. If we make wrong, rebellious choices, He'll allow these laws to affect us with consequences. God is love and a perfect gentleman. But He will not interfere if we don't acknowledge Him or want any part of Him in our lives.

He gave us authority to rule in our own individual lives by giving us the ability to choose. God will attempt to influence us into

JUDGING THE FRUIT OF RIGHTEOUSNESS • 93

making the right choices. However, we have a greater part to play in our own prosperity than most realize!

Only when we humble ourselves and seek His help will God intervene in our affairs, as 2 Chronicles 7:14 says. Consider the story of King Hezekiah. God paid him high compliments. The Bible states he did right in the eyes of the Lord, even as his father David had. This king destroyed idols, cleansed the temple, and restored worship there. He respected God's law and urged the people to obey it. When invaded by the king of Assyria, Hezekiah humbly turned to God for help and was delivered. However, later in life, his heart became proud and he was struck with a terminal illness, even to the point of death, described in 2 Chronicles 32:24-25.

It seemed all hope was gone. According to the natural laws of health, it was certain Hezekiah would die, because God allowed these laws to take affect in his body. Unless God intervened with divine power, natural laws would result in physical death.

God even sent Isaiah the prophet to warn the king to put his affairs in order, for he was about to die. He was told, "You will not recover." Hezekiah considered Isaiah a prophet who could be trusted to speak the Word of the Lord. He knew God's Word is the final authority and it will always come to pass.

Yet, he also realized God could change the natural laws of health for his dire situation. Despite words through Isaiah, Hezekiah believed he could persuade God to intervene. He remembered situations in Hebrew history when God showed mercy, because of prayer. So he pleaded his case before the Lord.

He asked God to remember all the times he had obeyed and led God's people to revival. Hezekiah specifically asked God to intervene and make an exception to the natural laws of this illness. Humbled, he wept bitterly. And our merciful God heard the prayers.

Isaiah had hardly left the palace when the Lord told him, "Go and tell Hezekiah that this is what the Lord God of your ancestor David says: I have heard your prayer; I have seen your tears. Look, I am going to add 15 years to your life." God intervened and spared a life.

During my own lifetime, I've heard numerous testimonies from believers of how God intervened to save them from negative circumstances. I've heard how people were delivered from drugs, the occult, pornography, homosexuality, disease, and other hopeless situations. Had the natural and spiritual laws continued in their lives without God's intervention, it more than likely would have resulted in prison, misery, suffering, or even death.

As revealed shortly in this chapter, God intervened in my own life too, when I was in my early twenties. I'm convinced, had God not helped me, nothing could have changed the negative physical and spiritual laws set in motion in my life. I'd have died prematurely at a very young age. He'll guide us if we ask and expect him to. He'll keep us out of trouble if we spend time listening to His wisdom and advice.

Many endure afflictions because they lack godly wisdom. We can get ourselves into trouble when we make wrong choices or say the wrong things. Sometimes this subjects us to unnecessary afflictions, but we cause it ourselves.

God will go to great lengths to warn us of our waywardness and spare us from unnecessary afflictions. While He doesn't force us to do His will, He will try to influence us through His Holy Spirit. In Old Testament times, God gave Israel the Law and sent His prophets to speak to His people. Today, under the new covenant, He speaks to us by the Holy Spirit, using the Bible as the guideline.

Those who've by faith repented of their sins and received Christ as Lord have the Spirit of Christ living within. Therefore, we have the inward witness of the Holy Spirit to teach us all things and guide us, as 1 John 2:27 says. God can speak to us through pastors, teachers, fellow believers, and even children. He appoints people to lead our nation to repentance. It doesn't necessarily have to be a preacher. He may use a doctor, movie producer, schoolteacher, musician, and even a politician to help influence the lives of others.

Persecutions and afflictions will indeed come to all of us—good and bad—because the earth is still in a fallen state. And we are all linked together on this earth; our choices, whether good or evil, will affect others. Adam's choice to disobey God brought a curse upon the earth. In contrast, Jesus' choice to obey God and endure the sufferings of the cross brought deliverance to all mankind. Adam's choice brought judgment and condemnation. But Jesus' choice brought justification. Through Adam's disobedience, death reigned. With Christ's obedience, life reigns within those who believe. Through Adam, one trespass brought condemnation to all men. Through Christ, one righteous act brought justification to all men, as it says in Romans 5:14-19.

While our choice doesn't carry the same weight as that of Adam and Jesus, the choices we make still affect our sphere of influence. A husband and father's choice to leave his family and pursue an adulterous affair affects all those near him. With his betrayal, he brings emotional pain and suffering to his wife. She feels rejected, unloved, unappreciated, and lonely. This, in turn, could lead her to a state of deep depression, which may affect her job performance.

The children feel angry and insecure from being abandoned. They may carry this anger with them into other relationships. Financial hardships usually ensue. In-laws also usually feel a sense of sadness, loss, shame, or enmity toward their relative's spouse. This adulterous relationship may leave an impression on some of his family and friends, who don't see its drastic consequences, that adultery is not so bad. It may influence others to take the same path of destruction.

His partner in adultery is also negatively affected, as well as her family, husband, and children, if she is married. She feels guilty, ashamed, and condemned. If married, her husband may go into an angry rage. No one in his or her sphere of influence is untouched.

A faithful husband and father affects those close to him, as well. His wife feels unconditionally loved, accepted, and appreciated. Her emotions are stable, at peace. He brings her joy and happiness. Although not perfect, he demonstrates through the years that he can be trusted.

He is a good provider and gives loving discipline to his children, so they are well trained and secure. When they get older, they remember his training, with self control and respect for others. They trust their parents to support them through high school and perhaps college. This father is an unselfish example.

During the years preceding World War II, Hitler, Mussolini, and Tojo made decisions which led to mass destruction of people and property. They made a choice to pursue power, grandeur, and the kingdoms of this world. The majority of people in those nations allowed them to rise in power and rule. These misguided leaders deceitfully pretended to negotiate for peace, all the while planning destruction.

The British and Europeans accepted Hitler's words of peace in good faith, not realizing he already had a battle strategy in place and had already planned to go forward with it. Japanese officials pretended to negotiate for peace with the USA, even as their bomber planes headed toward Pearl Harbor. The choice to use their elite armies for power and aggression affected the whole human race.

In contrast, Churchill, Roosevelt, and other allied leaders chose to oppose the evil powers of aggression in defense of freedom. These leaders courageously made tough decisions that halted Nazi aggression and Japanese imperialism. After WWII, the allied nations graciously extended a hand of friendship to their former enemies. They helped rebuild Germany, Japan, and Italy and ushered in long-lasting peace and goodwill with these nations. Now, instead of being a threat to peace, Germany, Italy, and Japan remain allies of peace.

Similarly, American leaders later decided to participate in negotiations with China and the Soviet Union. But the USA used the strength of a strong military presence to deter communist aggression. This resulted in an arms reduction and eventually led to the fall of the Iron Curtain. Decisions of righteous people bring prosperity, but decisions of the wicked bring evil.

Trials bring us to valleys of decision. We can choose to endure and allow afflictions to produce in us the fruit of righteousness, or we can allow persecutions to choke the Word of God and make us unfruitful. If we endure and submit unto God, these trials will help us to see how temporary life on earth is. Then we can begin to see what things in life are truly important and rearrange our priorities.

Of course, God would rather we prosper and allow Him to purify us with His word. He doesn't watch our every move, to see if we will make a mistake. He doesn't search for each tiny fault, to afflict or destroy us. God doesn't cause the affliction and suffering of the obedient who are in Christ. As we'll see in later chapters, He uses afflictions to keep us from going astray.

Some Bible teachers have gotten into needless debates over whether God *allows* or *causes* afflictions. Some believe God never causes afflictions, but allows them. Others believe God neither causes or allows afflictions, as if He never disciplines, or He's rarely involved in human affairs. There's no need for division or strife in this matter. The essential truth is that God judges individuals and nations by bringing afflictions, whether directly or indirectly.

He allows spiritual and physical laws to affect our lives, without directly interfering. For example, if someone jumped off a building to see if God's angels would save him, the law of gravity would take affect, giving him a hard landing—at best. God won't interfere, no matter how much faith the person thinks they have or how many times he or she confesses God's Word on the way down. God would not encourage and reward such a flagrant presumption. Another example is when Satan tempted Jesus, in Luke 4:9-12, to jump off the highest point of the temple in Jerusalem. Jesus refused, because He knew it would be tempting God to usurp the physical law of gravity.

For the most part, God allows His spiritual and physical laws to take affect without interfering. We can't plant apple seeds and expect pear trees to spring up. Similarly, we can't continually do evil deeds and expect God's blessings.

A more personal example is we can't sow seeds of laziness and expect to be wealthy. God won't interfere with spiritual laws and continually grant someone prosperity of any kind for doing nothing. He'll allow the lazy person to reap the affliction of poverty, so they'll learn the value of hard work.

Likewise, we can't continually abuse our bodies and expect God to bless us with health. One would be presumptuous to expect God to heal him of emphysema, yet continue heavy smoking. First, he must quit smoking, with God's help. Then, he can trust God to help him recover by natural, supernatural, and medical means. If a person rejects wisdom and continues to smoke, God may step aside and allow natural laws to take affect.

Others times we see from the Bible how God directly sent His angels to protect His covenant people by destroying whole cities and armies. If we sow bad seeds, with no knowledge of God, we'll reap bad seeds. If we live with little regard for God or His commandments, we will reap a rotten harvest. Always remember, God sees our lives here on earth from a different perspective than men. From His perspective, it's better to suffer in this life and enter into heaven than to live a life of comfort and ease, or evil, and suffer eternal death. *Eternal* death is *eternal* darkness! It's separation from God, far worse than any suffering of this present life!

> Before I was afflicted I went astray, but now I obey your word. You are good, and what you do is good; teach me your decrees.
> —Psalm 119:67-68

If we make disobedience choices we'll encounter trials and afflictions. In addition, our lack of divine wisdom will get us into more afflictions. Ignorance of God's commandments also leads us into many problems. Does God bring these afflictions? No, they come as a result of spiritual laws put into place before the world's foundation.

Much of the time, God will not interfere with these laws. He is a gentleman and won't force Himself into our lives. But when we break moral and spiritual laws, it will eventually result in problems. Nevertheless, God can use these situations to cleanse us and to bring us back onto the path of righteousness. Much of the results depend on our response.

My Personal Afflictions

Although God will not interfere with our choices, He might use suffering to purge us so we can bear more fruit. There were times in my life when I endured severe physical afflictions. Some of these came into my life as a result of natural laws, like neglect of my health. Others came through ignorance of God's Word. As a result, I found myself in serious problems.

As a young man attending college, I developed serious health problems. Although I loved the Lord, I had no knowledge of scriptures pertaining to healing, health, and faith. Neither did I have any knowledge concerning God's natural laws of health.

The year was 1979. The younger generation was awestruck by the Bee Gees, John Travolta, "Saturday Night Fever," and the disco scene. As a young college graduate, I had much graver concerns. I'd been suffering from chronic fatigue syndrome, and the summer prior to my senior year I was admitted into a hospital in Houston, Texas. It had a reputation for a few of the best doctors in the nation.

After extensive tests, they found abnormal results in my GI tract. But since they couldn't pinpoint the source of the problem, I returned home with little improvement. Although I continued to struggle with severe fatigue during my final college year, I managed to graduate at age 21 with honors in the Business Pre-law program from the University of Louisiana in Monroe.

I was readily admitted into Louisiana State University's Law School in Baton Rouge, where my oldest sister lived, along with her husband and children. They kindly offered for me to live in their home while I attended. Aspiring to one day become a judge, I looked forward to law school with great anticipation. Yet, because of persisting symptoms, there was also a dark cloud of fear that suffocated me with dread.

Throughout my early childhood, I had endured many diseases including severe allergies, malaria, rheumatic fever, pneumonia, and ulcers. This resulted in a stronghold of fear in my life at an early age. By the time I finished college, I had been on antibiotics, allergy shots, and antihistamines for most of my childhood, teenage, and young adult years. I thought, perhaps I could get a much-needed rest during the summer, then be ready for fall semester.

One hot, sultry Louisiana bayou day in August, I made my way across the university campus. As I walked through each stage of registration, I felt greater and greater fatigue. The tiredness I'd experienced during undergraduate school plagued me again, but it seemed much worse in the South Louisiana humidity. Nevertheless, I plodded on, determined to beat the steamy afternoon and complete registration.

I'll drink some water, and I'll be fine, I thought, reassuring myself. But soon, nausea joined the fatigue. I finally completed my tasks and sat on a bench, under one of the beautiful, huge, moss-covered cedar trees.

"God, please help me get back to the house," I remember saying in a brief prayer.

To my relief, I did make it home and retired early that evening. Tomorrow was my important first day of classes. As I lay in bed, I felt each beat of my heart. The palpitations pounded in my chest. So needless to say, I had a troubled, sleepless night.

The next morning as the alarm screamed, I sat up in bed. Although my palpitations had subsided, I felt dizzy and ill, as if I was poisoned. I opened my eyes in the pitch dark, walked across the bedroom, feeling the walls, then flipping the light switch. But to my dismay, it remained dark. Horror gripped me as I slowly realized I couldn't see.

I called out in panic until my sister and her husband arrived in the bedroom. My five or ten minutes of darkness seemed hours. Eventually, my eyesight did gradually begin to return. But my sister took me to the emergency room anyway; my mom drove down from northern Louisiana.

Physicians ran extensive tests but were unable to detect my problem. Even though I had lost about forty pounds during the previous year's illnesses, they released me from the hospital a week later, without a diagnosis. Some suspected the incident was stress induced, and I continued to be under a physician's care. But this wasn't the end of the trial.

Because I had missed the first week of law school, the dean recommended I wait and return next fall. But I never did begin studying law. I spent almost a year recovering at my parents' home, a farm in northern Louisiana. Then I finally landed a job at my former undergraduate university and later transferred to a computer-programming job in Baton Rouge.

Still, I was extremely fatigued, and struggled to keep up my job performance. I suffered numerous ear and sinus infections.

A mental cloudiness continued to inhibit my concentration. And except for no future episodes of blindness, my various symptoms persisted for the next four years, sometimes improving, sometimes getting worse.

My hopes and dreams now shattered, my priorities in life began to change. No longer did it seem important to have a date for the weekend. It didn't matter who won the Super Bowl or the World Series, and I lost interest in favorite television shows.

Friends and family helped me as much as humanly possible, but they could not heal me, nor could the doctors help me. Problems developed with my job; rude drivers irritated me in traffic; family relational issues grew. It seemed everywhere I turned, devils used someone or something to attack and wear me down.

For several years I struggled—every day—for energy to get out of bed and go to work! It was, for me, an act of great faith to merely crawl out of my bed. My social life came to a screeching halt! Friends asked me to go out with them, and I had to turn them down. Siblings were busy with their children and jobs, and everyone else busied themselves with the cares and activities of life.

So, living alone as a single young man, I found nowhere to turn for help or comfort. I spiraled into a pit of depression. I finally came to a point of hopelessness and deep desperation. I asked God to either heal me or take me home.

Then, for the first time in my life, I turned completely to God and began to spend quality time with Him. God finally had my full, undivided attention. Through reading and meditation on His Word, I began not only to learn *about* God, but also to *know* Him in a close, personal way. I began to fellowship.

Soon, He revealed principles in His Word I had never seen before. He revealed my idols. But He also strengthened and encouraged me and showed me his promises. And gradually, He released me from the "rat race" of my life. Now, like I dwelt high above the earth, in God's presence, I seemed to watch from outside daily, busy pressures most adults face.

I came to realize things of the world that once held my attention were only empty shells of discontentment. I discovered the most exciting treasure known to man. I found the kingdom of God.

During this trying time of affliction, God produced in me the peaceable fruit of righteousness. Was it God's perfect will for me to suffer? I think not. But before this affliction, I did *not* walk in His perfect plan for my life. Sure, I went to church on Sundays, but I hardly gave God a second thought during the rest of the week. I had developed strongholds of sin in my mind and needed deliverance.

Was it God's will for me to be in bondage? Most certainly not! Why then did He allow this? After all, I was a born-again Christian. Yet I gradually and finally understood that afflictions result from man's fallen state and from choices made.

Although I considered myself a believer, I didn't take time to meditate daily in the Holy Scriptures. I lived ignorant of many principles in the kingdom of God. And there were certain truths that I absolutely avoided, or did not believe applied today!

> Before I was afflicted I went astray, but now I obey your word.
> You are good, and what you do is good; teach me your decrees.
> —Psalm 119:67-68

Before this severe trial, I bore little fruit, good or bad. I wasn't notoriously evil or perverted. However, I pursued only selfish interests, thinking little of others. I never thought of anyone outside of my own little box. I went to church on Sundays, but had little interest in the Bible and seldom prayed. I spent most of my spare time watching secular television and pursuing entertainment. I gave little thought to the kingdom of God.

I had little concern for other poor, wretched souls who were hungry, destitute, and bound by the darkness of evil. I had little compassion for those held captive by sin. Besides, how could I help others when I had my own strongholds of sin that I'd never fully dealt with?

I was overcome by fear, too shy to reach out and enjoy or love others. I could be in a room full of people for hours, and no one even noticed I was there. But then, I didn't want them to notice me. My fears and insecurity made me want to hide.

To bear fruit, we must abide in Christ, as John 15:5 says. But I'd never taken the time to spend with Christ, nor did I have much desire to abide in Him. Now, though, I spent most of my time in prayer and Bible study. So I began to understand more of God's character and the kind of fruit God expects a good tree to produce. I finally began to contemplate the purpose for which I was born, as He brought me to a point of total humility and absolute surrender.

Throat infections, ear infections, and mental cloudiness continued to affect my job performance, threatening my security. My strength was still totally depleted. I felt as if I could hardly move, as though I were in an utterly helpless state. Doctors remained bewildered as to the source of my illness. In their opinion, there was nothing they could do. I felt like the woman in Mark 5:26 with the flowing blood, who spent all she had on many physicians, yet grew worse.

Who could I turn to except God? I abandoned my hopes, dreams, and future into His hands. I prayed in earnest, "Not my will, but your will be done in my life," as Jesus did in Matthew 26:39.

As I began to seek the Lord, He revealed the importance of trusting and believing His promises. As my pride was cast down, I discovered I had been wrong in some beliefs. I had no idea of God's calling upon my life or the events He had in store. However, I began to learn how God speaks directly to us, individually, through His Word. I began to hear God's voice by meditating in the Bible and listening to my conscience.

After a couple of years had passed, God's Spirit impressed on my conscience, "I will raise you up." Still, several more years passed without any significant medical improvement.

"You will live, not die. I will raise you up to declare the works of the Lord," the Holy Spirit persisted.

And God did. Beginning July 16, 1981, He set me on a road to recovery and gave me new direction—a day I will never forget! It was the day I made a determined commitment to live by faith.

"Mark this day on your calendar and always remember it. This day you will begin your journey of faith," the Holy Spirit impressed on my mind.

I didn't receive a miraculous, instantaneous healing. It was a gradual recovery, which required faith, patience, and endurance. But on that day I made a choice to live by faith, a choice which would change my life. I had looked to physicians for healing, as if they were gods. And I discovered they were only human. I learned to follow the voice of the Holy Spirit, in my conscience.

"Listen to your body. It will show you what to do," He said.

Then I noticed every time I took an antibiotic, I felt more physically drained. I began to gradually omit antibiotics. My sore throat symptoms and fever persisted, but I realized that returning down the road of past failed attempts to improve my health was useless. So I stayed off antibiotics, trusting that my God-given immunity system, along with the healing power of God's word, would bring health.

Next, I noticed whenever I ate refined sugar, fatigue and mental cloudiness increased, so I cut out all sweets, except for natural fruit. I also was compelled to make sure my food was fresh. So I began to check expiration dates.

Then I also noticed breads irritated my symptoms. So I abstained from all yeast products. After taking each of these steps, I noticed gradual but steady improvement.

A few years later, I learned from a friend that new medical research described a condition called Candida, fungi that resemble yeast. This condition can arise from overuse of antibiotics. In the most severe cases, it can produce extreme fatigue and cause symptoms similar to alcohol intoxication, even poisoning. I finally understood the causes for my medical problems over the past few years.

Let me emphatically state that I'm not against doctors and medicines. I'll still use both occasionally. However, it becomes dangerous if we abuse medications and trust in them more than God.

God used physical conditions to clarify my life and interests, so I could eventually bear fruit. I began to pray for others and witness at work, mostly through my lifestyle. But I did unashamedly share my Christian faith. Later, as my health gradually improved, I got involved in church outreach, started singing in the college and career choir, and participated in church visitation. Through my adult Sunday school class I helped in a nursing home and a battered-children's shelter.

Then finally, at age twenty-five, something most wonderful happened that radically altered the course of my life. On the day of Pentecost in 1983, quite unexpectedly, I was filled with the fullness of the Holy Spirit. Afterwards, God's Word burned in my heart like never before.

Traditional old hymns seemed to leap off their pages. I had sung these since early childhood, but never saw the beautiful worship behind each verse and chorus. The zeal of God consumed me. My prayer life went from shallow and empty duty to words of power and faith. From being a shy, introverted person, I now spoke with boldness the wonderful works of Christ. I'd been utterly depressed, in a constantly sad state of mind; now I felt unspeakable joy.

Family, friends, and fellow employees saw the difference and were amazed. Instead of always being unnoticed, as in the past, the Holy Spirit drew others to me. People approached me, striking up conversations. But my newfound power and influence brought new persecution, as well.

Looking back, I realize what a great work God did in those tough years, which I certainly have no desire to endure again. However, those difficult times forever changed my life and destiny. From that time forward, I always felt aware of God's presence in tangible ways, though my life has not been perfect.

Did God desire I go though sickness and afflictions? I think not. Rather, a lack of knowledge about God's spiritual principals, as well as little understanding of God's natural laws concerning health, brought my troubles. So He used them to purify me and gave me a testimony of His goodness and grace.

Why are some people not healed? I don't know and don't pretend to have all the answers. Yet, I know God *can* deliver us from trials, no matter how hopeless our circumstances. Christ desires to heal and restore everyone. But we have a part to play in our prosperity.

A lack of knowledge can result in trials and afflictions. Jordan Rubin, in his best-selling book, *The Maker's Diet,* expounds on God's natural and spiritual laws of health. Rubin emphasizes healing for man's spirit, soul, and body. What we receive into our spirit, soul, and body significantly determines our well being.

As examples of modern ways to entertain "garbage," consider the following scenarios:

- If you eat junk food, excessive amounts of sugars and preservatives, and favor the unclean foods the Creator warned us about, then you will almost certainly reap an unpleasant harvest of failed health later in life.

- If your friends and close associates are people who use "recreational" drugs, get drunk, and are promiscuous, then you are likely to fall into a very dangerous lifestyle yourself sooner or later.
- If you fill your mind with unhealthy and unwholesome images of pornography, violence, fractured relationships, and scornful attitudes about God, eternal values, and godly living, you will begin to act out what you put in.[1]

Disobedience will also result in afflictions. We cannot expect to prosper if we continue to live in disobedience. God loves a rebellious person, even when they have nothing to do with Him. Rebellion blinds people to God's goodness. They invite affliction, while He desires to heal and restore them. But they refuse to listen. The only way out of affliction is to end rebellion and return to the Lord. But if we seek Him, He'll help us through our afflictions.

God may still purge us by allowing us to face the natural consequences of our wrongdoings, but He will help us endure, with grace. Facing consequences and being held accountable builds our character. Although painful to our pride and flesh, this type of purging is another act of God's love.

The only way to prosperity is to love righteousness and obey His commandments, which bring His revelation. Obedience opens our eyes and our understanding to God's goodness, justice, omniscience, faithfulness, and integrity. A revelation, a new, deep understanding of the Messiah will bring prosperity. Yet we must also consider: are all afflictions the result of disobedience and rebellion?

SHEEP FOR THE SLAUGHTER

Scripture examples are clear: all sickness is *not* a result of a person's sins or ignorance. Every trial is not the result of a person's sins or failures. Sometimes afflictions occur in fulfillment of God's plan for our lives.

All children born into the world are important to God. Sometimes God uses seemingly impossible trials and circumstances involving children to bring about their destiny, to bring about His will on the earth. When hellish forces contend with God over the lives of children through various means, maybe they know that child has a divine destiny to fulfill.

For example, notice how many of the great characters of the Bible endured adverse circumstances at their birth. Somehow, the principalities of darkness knew when these children of destiny were about to be born. Perhaps Satan examined prophecy and heard what the prophets said concerning their births, or he got word of angelic announcements, which occurred over the births of men like Samson, John the Baptist, Isaac, and, of course, Jesus. It is evident Satan knows the Holy Scriptures, because he quoted them to Jesus when he tempted Him in the wilderness in Luke 4:9-11.

Children of promise such as Isaac, Samson, Samuel, and John the Baptist all had this one thing common: their parents were barren for many years. Children were targeted again when the powers of hell influenced Pharaoh to kill all the Hebrew babies. Apparently they knew from prophecy in Genesis 15:13-14 that a deliverer, Moses, was about to be born.

Likewise, the gospels tell how King Herod ordered all males two and under to be slaughtered, in an attempt to kill the Messiah. But these children of promise survived, each to fulfill his destiny. God was always one step ahead of the devil, and so He is today!

Afflictions may arise even when people obey. Does God bring it? No, He does not. Satan is the destroyer. Many times affliction comes when we *obey* the Holy Spirit. As we've discussed, Satan and his evil subordinates want to stop us from bearing good fruit. So if afflictions come for righteousness sake, God will use them to bring us to a closer walk with Him.

"Your most profound and intimate experiences of worship will likely be in your darkest days—when your heart is broken, when you feel abandoned, when you're out of options, when the pain is great—and you turn to God alone."[2]

God doesn't cause our darkness, either. Nevertheless, God will use it to strengthen us so we can bear more fruit. Again, the speed and intensity of the results may depend on our speed and intensity to respond.

Hebrews 5:8 states Jesus learned obedience by what He suffered. He was baptized by John the Baptist and filled with the Holy Spirit. Then the Spirit led Him into the wilderness to be tempted.

I can't imagine it would be any fun to go without food for forty days and forty nights in the wilderness. Yet, this is precisely what the Holy Spirit led Jesus to do. And by gross understatement, it wasn't a pleasure to suffer a horrific death on a cross. Yet this affliction Jesus had to endure.

Did the Father crucify Him? Did He *cause* it? God forbid! Nevertheless, the Father knew what would occur when He sent His Son to earth as a baby. He knew of Jesus' torture and death. But it pleased God for Jesus to suffer and be put to death, so he could rise again on the third day, defeating death forever!

How is God pleased at the suffering of his beloved seed? He knew His Son's death provided many more adopted sons. Under God's spiritual laws of the universe, it was the only way to reconcile mankind to Himself. God sowed His Son into the world to reap a harvest of sons and daughters. Jesus was destined to be a holy sacrifice for men's sins. It is for this divine purpose He came into the world.

Outside of our Lord Jesus Christ, there is no better example of afflictions from obedience than the great Apostle Paul. His life was also one of sacrifice. Because of revelations he received and the call upon his life, a messenger of Satan caused strife and trouble everywhere he went. Paul traveled from town to town, preaching the gospel of Jesus Christ, with supernatural results. Many believed in Jesus. Then Satan stirred up trouble. As a result, Paul was often run out of town.

Paul describes it in his second letter to the Corinthians, when he confronted those who tried to corrupt the simplicity of Christ's saving death and resurrection. Perhaps unknowingly, these teachers had strayed from truth. They questioned and undermined Paul's authority from Jesus. Maybe Paul's physical appearance and manner didn't measure up to what they judged to be an Apostle. So Paul defends his authority, and in the process describes his hardships, caused by a messenger of Satan.

> Are they Hebrews? So am I. Are they Israelites? So am I. Are they Abraham's descendants? So am I. Are they servants of Christ? (I am out of my mind to talk like this.) I am more. I have worked much harder, been in prison more frequently, been flogged more severely, and been exposed to death again and again. Five times I received from the Jews the forty lashes minus one. Three times I was beaten with rods; once I was stoned; three times I was shipwrecked; I spent a night and a day in the open sea; I have been constantly on the move. I have been in danger from rivers, in danger from bandits, in danger from my own countrymen, in danger from Gentiles; in danger in the city, in danger in the country, in danger at sea; and in danger from false brothers. I have labored and toiled and have often gone without sleep; I have known hunger and thirst and have often gone without food; I have been cold and naked. Besides everything else, I face daily the pressure of my concern for all the churches.
> —2 Corinthians 11:22-28

Notice how Paul equates persecution and suffering with authority. He seems to imply greater sacrifice and suffering with greater authority. Some people imply Paul endured hardships because he didn't have a revelation to understand a believer's authority, like we do today. But this idea contradicts Scripture.

Paul's eyes were blinded by Christ's glory on the road to Damascus. In Acts 9:15-16, the Lord instructed Ananias to lay hands on Paul, and he would receive his sight. Ananias acted overly cautious. Paul had a long reputation for zealous persecution of Christians. He didn't realize that the exact persecution he inflicted upon believers, he'd endure in the future himself—and more. Jesus reassured Ananias and revealed to him the Apostle Paul's impending distresses.

> But the Lord said to Ananias, "Go! This man is my chosen instrument to carry my name before the Gentiles and their kings and before the people of Israel. *I will show him how much he must suffer for my name.*"
>
> —Acts 9:15-16

So we have to consider a question, did Paul suffer because he didn't have a revelation of the believer's authority? And if so, why did Jesus say Paul must suffer for His name's sake? Paul walked in the same authority as any believer of Christ. It seems, from reading the book of Acts and his letters to the churches, Paul had a good understanding of the believer's authority in Christ. He cast out devils, healed the sick, and preached with authority. Paul endured great suffering as a chosen vessel. He was able to, since he committed himself and his appointed work to the Faithful One.

> And of this gospel I was appointed a herald and an apostle and a teacher. That is why I am suffering as I am. Yet I am not ashamed,

because I know whom I have believed, and am convinced that he is able to guard what I have entrusted to him for that day.
—2 Timothy 1:11-12

Paul's zeal for Christ drew Satan's attention and resulting afflictions because of His faith and revelation. Satan will oppose revelation and anointing from whomever it flows.

To keep me from becoming conceited because of these surpassingly great revelations, there was given me a thorn in my flesh, a messenger of Satan, to torment me. Three times I pleaded with the Lord to take it away from me. But he said to me, "My grace is sufficient for you, for my power is made perfect in weakness." Therefore I will boast all the more gladly about my weaknesses, so that Christ's power may rest on me. That is why, for Christ's sake, I delight in weaknesses, in insults, in hardships, in persecutions, in difficulties. For when I am weak, then I am strong.
—2 Corinthians 12:7-10

How could Paul take pleasure in weakness, reproach, necessities, persecution, and distress? With the power of his revelation: "When I am weak, then am I strong." In our weaknesses, we come to God as little, helpless children and take hold of His power within us. In feeling our reproaches, we understand Christ's sufferings.

Accordingly, we also look to Him for love and acceptance. In daily necessities, we learn to trust Him and receive by faith. Through persecution, we learn endurance and forgiveness. And we learn to maintain a calm spirit, overcome fear, and walk as God's children when in distress. In our weaknesses, we are made strong. Therefore we can say as Paul did in 2 Corinthians 12:9: "Therefore I will boast all the more gladly about my weaknesses, so that Christ's power may rest on me."

This explains why Paul willingly endured hardship and imprisonment; why he was stoned and went right back into the same town to encourage those in the faith. It is why he could endure hunger, nakedness, beatings, storms, and shipwrecks without giving up or quitting. He knew that in his weakness, the Spirit of Christ made him strong. He realized God worked all of his hardships for good. He persevered with the gospel, finally preaching in Rome, even to Caesar.

Paul did not fear suffering for God's kingdom; he knew Christ's power rested upon him. He realized God worked in him through circumstances. Paul knew these afflictions were only temporary, and God used him to light the darkness of sin with the glorious gospel. Through these afflictions, God perfected Paul.

So it is with all who abide in Christ, within whom His Holy Spirit rests. We are not afraid to take a stand against anything that is contrary to God's commandments. We are not afraid what others think when we refuse to participate in the works of darkness. We are not concerned when others slander us unjustly. We are not afraid to endure hardships for His name's sake.

Like Paul in Romans 8:18, we *can* say, "None of these things move me." We'll show compassion to the humble, poor, and needy. We'll forgive those who wrong us. We will boldly proclaim His truth and defend His righteous cause. We'll be willing to endure affliction.

Our obedience brings God's revelation and opens our eyes and our understanding to His goodness. Once we see that, we can stand in faith and trust in His goodness, even in the midst of the most severe afflictions we can imagine.

Cut Down and Cast into Fire

Notice that every good tree that does not bring forth good fruit is cut down and cast into the fire. John the Baptist preached these same words.

> The ax is already at the root of the trees, and every tree that does not produce good fruit will be cut down and thrown into the fire.
> —Luke 3:9

Producing good fruit is significant to God. *God is the Great Fruit Inspector!* And those who grow good fruit are trimmed, for strength, so they can bear more. Those who are *not* fruitful are cut down and cast into fire. Earlier in the chapter, we discussed how God purges us so we will bear more fruit. Let's turn our attention to those who are cut away and burned. Jesus also teaches the importance of fruit in John's gospel, which gives us further insight concerning good and bad fruit.

> I am the true vine, and my Father is the gardener. He cuts off every branch in me that bears no fruit, while every branch that does bear fruit he prunes so that it will be even more fruitful. You are already clean because of the word I have spoken to you. Remain in me, and I will remain in you. No branch can bear fruit by itself; it must remain in the vine. Neither can you bear fruit unless you remain in me. I am the vine; you are the branches. If a man remains in me and I in him, he will bear much fruit; apart from me you can do nothing. *If anyone does not remain in me, he is like a branch that is thrown away and withers; such branches are picked up, thrown into the fire and burned.* If you remain in me and my words remain in you, ask whatever you wish, and it will be given you. This is to my Father's glory, that you bear much fruit, showing yourselves to be my disciples.
> —John 15:1-8

In John's gospel, Jesus tells us how to produce fruit: We must abide in Christ. What does that mean? How do we abide or remain in Christ?

When we spend time in prayer, worship, and fellowship with other believers, we abide. To abide in Christ means to spend time in His Word. Christ's teaching cleans and purges us, then we'll produce more fruit. The Apostle Paul had learned to abide in Christ. As a result, he declared, "When I am weak, then am I strong."

Some people argue that setting time aside each day to study the Word of God is legalistic. I ask, "How much fruit do you produce?" Granted, we do not have to be legalistic and rigid in our schedule for Bible study. However, the only way to bring forth fruit is to abide in Christ, which means spending time in His Word, reading His thoughts. Christ is our Living Word. So it doesn't seem legalistic to set time aside each day for prayer and meditation; rather, it seems a necessity! Indeed, God's Word is our entire life. Without Christ, the Living Word, we can do nothing, as John 15:5 says.

If we fail to abide in Christ, we are like a branch cut off a vine, without nourishment, without life. We soon wither and die. When a branch dies, it is cut away. And who trims out dead wood? Not God; men do. A person who ceases to multiply fruit will be removed and incinerated. These scriptures show a correlation between good fruit and God's divine protection.

I'm not implying all tragedies are a result of fruitless lives. As previously mentioned, many people go through adverse circumstances precisely when they *are* doing a mighty work for the Lord. Sometimes, the powers of darkness come to oppose them, as they did Paul.

On the other hand, there are those who *do* endure sorrow due to fruitless lives. When we cease to abide in Christ, we cease to yield good fruit. When we cease to produce, we lose God's presence and in turn, His divine protection. What is a dead, dried up branch good for, except as fuel in a fire? A fire of God's judgment is an example to children of disobedience. We can be sure; those who cease fruitfulness will fall under God's judgment. God will give them over to evil men for destruction.

> You are the salt of the earth. But if the salt loses its saltiness, how can it be made salty again? It is no longer good for anything, except to be thrown out and trampled by men.
> —Matthew 5:13

Jesus speaks to believers here. Christians are to flavor the earth with righteousness, truth, and holiness. We are to produce compassion, goodness, and kindness. If we lose our flavor, we lose God's divine protection. Unless we repent and begin to provide fruit, we'll be trampled under by cruel men and extinguished by flames. We can see from Jesus how important it is to produce righteousness. Sometimes we open ourselves up to afflictions because we cease fruitful living, like we once did.

THE GREAT FRUIT INSPECTOR

We see another example of the importance of bearing fruit in the parable of financial "talents," in Matthew 25:14-30. In this parable, Jesus tells a story of a man who traveled to a far country. No doubt the man referred to is Himself. At this point, Jesus knew He was about to leave His disciples and give His life as a ransom for the world's sins.

In this parable, a man travels to a far country and leaves his possessions at home for his servants to care for while he is away. He gives five talents to one servant, two to a second, and one to a third servant. These talents were given to produce fruit for God's kingdom.

Christ is in the people business; He loves and cares for humans. As our Good Shepherd, His possessions are His sheep. And He wants sheep who obey, and others who protect and guide them.

The first two servants bore fruit. However, the servant with one talent hid it and pursued pleasures and entertainment. He cared nothing for his master's possessions, but only about himself. After a long time, the master returned and dealt with them. He commends the first two for using their money wisely.

In contrast, he rebukes the third servant, calling him wicked and lazy. He took away this man's talent and gave it to another, showing in essence: You should have used your talent to bear fruit. The master judged this servant unprofitable and orders him cast into outer darkness.

Notice that Jesus calls all three of these men servants. We have all observed those who claim to be Christians, through the years, who backslide and lose their effectiveness as a believer and a witness. A backslider's miserable life is a sad sight. Other Christians may reach out to help a backslider, but they refuse all help. Now deceived, they are enticed into seduction of the flesh and they cease to produce good fruit. They appear to no longer want anything to do with Christ or the kingdom of God.

We have all watched someone continue on their destructive path. But others bent on sin repent and are saved from trampled destruction. Yet some are cut down in their prime, destroyed.

It could happen to any of us if we do not stay alert, as 1 Peter 5:8 says. If we do not abide in Christ, we tend to drift in a strong current of lethargy. If we are not awakened and brought to our senses, John 15:6 makes it clear this strong pull will draw us under to our death. Unless we repent, crying out to God, we will be cast into darkness, to drown in a sea of heartache and destruction. We must abide in Christ. If we lose our saltiness, men will trample us.

Another example of fruitfulness is found in a parable of the husbandmen, in Matthew 21:33-41. A land owner planted a vineyard, dug a winepress, and built a tower. He laid a good foundation for the harvest. The owner sacrificed much time, labor, and expense. He then loaned his vineyard to husbandmen or sharecroppers.

When the time for harvest drew near, the owner sent his servants to receive fruit from his vineyard. But the husbandmen received these servants, beat one, killed another, and stoned a third. So the owner sent more servants, who met the same results. Finally, the owner sent his son thinking, *Surely they will respect him.*

But when they saw the owner's son arrive, they did not want to give what belonged to him. So, believing they could steal the son's inheritance, the husbandmen threw the son from the vineyard and killed him also, as they had done to his servants.

"When the Lord of the vineyard comes, what will he do to those husbandmen?" Jesus asked.

The vineyard in this parable represents God's possessions. These include the earth and His people. God has loaned the earth to mankind. And God expects us to take care of it, as well as take care of His people. He will hold us accountable for what we do with His possessions on loan during His absence.

While absent from the earth, God has sent His prophets to investigate what fruit the husbandmen of His earth produce. Examples are in Nehemiah 1:1-7; Proverbs 1:31; Isaiah 3:10-11; Jeremiah 6:19, 9:2-9, 16:17-18; Hosea 10:12; Amos 6:12; Jonah 1:1-2; Matthew 3:8.

God is the Great Fruit Inspector! He inspects our lives, thoughts, and deeds. Needless to say, the Pharisees produced corrupt fruit. God sent many prophets to rebuke them and hold them accountable. But the Pharisees mistreated, ridiculed, pummeled, and even killed God's voices. Next, God sent His son. But they esteemed Him lightly. After all, He never trained in their theology schools. He was merely a carpenter's son, trying to usurp their authority and steal the people's hearts. So they murdered Him as well.

Luke 6:26 tells us God is not concerned with how popular we are with men. He does not judge us by how wealthy we are. Nor does he judge by worldly status and power, as we see in Mark 9:34-37 and Matthew 16:26. This one thing is essential to God: What fruit do we produce?

Even today, God inspects the earth and sends His servants to speak on His behalf. They preach repentance and salvation through the Messiah, Jesus Christ. They stand and speak God's truth and righteousness. God uses them to rebuke and warn of future judgments. Yet God's messengers are ridiculed and mistreated, like in the past. In some nations they are murdered. Still, God, who owns the universe, will one day return and deal with these husbandmen. When He sees how we've treated His possessions, what will He say and do?

Our Divine Destiny is to Judge

We see from Scripture the importance to give a good harvest. But what role do we as Christians have in judging fruit?

In order to establish God's righteousness on this earth, God's children must be able to judge. When we speak of judging, it means an ability to discern where people are in their relationship with God. Then we can help them overcome sin and live an abundant life in fellowship with their Creator.

Judging also involves ruling. Because His Holy Spirit lives within us, one day believers will rule and reign with Christ. If we rule and reign with Christ, we must have the ability to judge.

> If any of you has a dispute with another, dare he take it before the ungodly for judgment instead of before the saints? Do you not know that the saints will judge the world? And if you are to judge the world, are you not competent to judge trivial cases?

> Do you not know that we will judge angels? How much more the things of this life!
> —I Corinthians 6:1-3

As we see from these scriptures, God's servants are given wisdom, discernment, and a responsibility to judge. But an erroneous teaching exists that implies we, as Christians, cannot judge. On the contrary, God's people have the Supreme Judge, even the Spirit of Wisdom, living within us. As a matter of fact, we all make judgments.

Webster's Dictionary defines judge: "To form an opinion about through careful weighing of evidence and testing of premises; to govern or rule; to form an estimate or evaluation of; to form an opinion."[3]

From this definition, we know everyone judges. People of all ages, religions, and nations have their own opinions. World leaders, professionals, educated, uneducated, housewives, and children all have their opinions. Examples vary from those who render an historical opinion on the Supreme Court to children sizing up their classmates. We all form opinions!

Good citizens judge when they cast their vote in an election. Without judgment, anarchy and chaos would prevail. Judgment *must* be rendered, to prevent lawlessness! However, there is a wrong and a right way to judge.

God expects the Church to judge in righteousness, by wisdom from the Holy Spirit. We are to judge in the everyday affairs of our lives, our families, our church, and our government. Judgment involves rendering decisions based on opinions. As Christians, our decisions should be rendered based on the Bible. In order to judge justly, we must be filled with God's Word and therefore His Spirit of Wisdom. Before we can even begin to judge in a worthy manner, we must judge ourselves. Then we will see properly, justly, in order to judge others.

> But if we judged ourselves, we would not come under judgment. When we are judged by the Lord, we are being disciplined so that we will not be condemned with the world.
> —I Corinthians 11:31-32

Once again we see the Lord's goodness in judgment. God judges his children so we will not be condemned along with this evil world. Paraphrasing what Jesus said, if your hand causes you to sin, cut it off. For it is better to enter into heaven with no hand than condemned with the world and lose your soul.

We must judge ourselves first, so we are not condemned with the world. This doesn't mean we should always feel condemned or get into legalistic bondage. But we should, as the Apostle Paul said, "Work out our salvation with fear and trembling," (Philippians 2:12).

In other words, we should always work toward holiness, willing to receive correction and quick to repent. When we fear our Lord, we begin to judge ourselves. When we judge ourselves, we gain wisdom and understanding. Only then are we able to judge others.

> Do not judge, and you will not be judged. Do not condemn, and you will not be condemned. Forgive, and you will be forgiven.
> —Luke 6:37

Many people misinterpret these words of Christ to say Christians should not judge, ever, at all! However, this would contradict other scriptures, which state believers will rule with Christ and judge nations. The word "judge" in Luke 6:37 implies to judge in a condemning manner.[4] It implies to judge in a harsh, hypocritical way, without forgiveness. But Jesus teaches we are to always judge in mercy. Though we do not condone evil actions of others, we are also commanded to forgive as God, for Christ's sake, has forgiven us.

> ...because judgment without mercy will be shown to anyone who has not been merciful. Mercy triumphs over judgment!
> —James 2:13

At this point, our Lord cautions us in how we judge others. We must keep in mind, were it not for Christ's merciful power, we could live in the lowest pit of sin. We should always look at others with the compassion of Christ. No person is so evil Christ cannot save and change them. If we judge without mercy, we will receive judgment without mercy. From the words of Jesus and James, we see principles of sowing and reaping in the area of judgment.

How Do We Judge?

How do we as Christians administer righteousness and justice? Are we to take up our guns and force everyone to repent? Do we protest in the streets with picket signs about bad actions of people? Do we yell and scream at them and say they will go to hell?

We, as Christ's disciples, are not to judge in our natural strength, but in His Spirit. We are not to take God's laws into our own hands or attempt to enforce laws ourselves. Rather we are to enforce God's laws through the spiritual realm of prayer, speaking His Word over Christians through circumstances. In addition, we judge by working to ensure godly authorities rule in our nation.

A good way to entwine morality into a nation is to change people's hearts through our lives and persuasive discussion. But our most effective weapon is wielded on our knees, crying out to God on behalf of the wicked. Another effective tool is to vote godly people into leadership.

Godly leaders will pass laws based on the Word of God. Then godly judges will interpret these laws in light of God's Word. Once good laws are passed, with judges who interpret them correctly, we obviously need a godly president who will enforce these laws. We cannot and are not to bring about changes by physical force, but by entrusting ourselves unto God, who is faithful and just.

For instance, we are not to fight against abortion by killing doctors. We are not to render bodily harm to those whom we may feel deserve punishment. Rather, we are to pray for them, speak out kindly, and entrust the situation into God's hands. Through the power of prayer, some of these doctors who take away life could become givers of life! Some of the most godless judges could be born again and become the wisest in administrating justice.

As Martin Luther King, Jr. worked to promote civil rights for African Americans, so are we to aggressively take a stand against abortion through peaceful means. Once laws prohibit abortions, God will use the authorities to enforce them. We should refrain from physically enforcing laws ourselves, and allow those placed in government authority to use force, if necessary, to protect innocent lives, as Romans 13:3 says. A wonderful aspect of democracy is it allows God's people to rise up and play an active role in their nation's destiny. This is the correct and wise way for Christians to judge.

As Christians, it is our responsibility to take an active role in judging and ruling. We are to judge with mercy, humbly remembering how God has brought us from darkness into His marvelous light.

A person's fruit, whether good or bad, will affect all aspects of his life. Whether we believe and practice the Bible or not determines what fruit we produce. And what seeds we sow, whether good or bad, affects our home, work, hobbies, and our nation. What we do and say springs from what we believe or don't believe. Our actions, words, and thoughts flow from what's within our heart, our mind.

A person's heart influences where he stands on national issues and how he votes. Those who lack knowledge in righteousness, or any who reject God's commandments, will vote for corrupt leaders and stand for immoral issues. Corrupt leaders will in turn appoint judges void in the wisdom of truth.

Some judges in our nation are ignorant of justice, because they don't seek the Just One to give them wisdom. Even now, some federal judges render decisions contrary to the written Word of God. By these unrighteous decisions, we see the fruit they produce. Are we to obey anything contrary to the Scriptures? Are we to obey what violates our conscience?

Of course, we are to obey the laws of our land if they do not violate God's commandments, which carry more weight than manmade edicts. The prophets of old judged evil kings in their day. John the Baptist judged King Herod for living with his brother's wife. We also are not to be cowardly and allow evil to rule without comment.

We are to work diligently to change evil in government, where honorable men and women hold many offices. Nevertheless, some do not respect God or His justice. And some courts today have a twisted sense of justice.

Some judges are so full of pride; they never admit they are wrong. They defy congress and the people by rewriting or creating new statutes instead of interpreting them. Others seem to believe common people are too ignorant to know right from wrong. It's amazing, but a judge may spend years studying men's laws, yet remain unable to discern truth! This is because they have neither seen God, nor have they known Him. Judges blind to truth sit on their thrones and treat God's commandments with contempt.

We can only see God through His written Word, through His Son's life, and through His Holy Spirit. And as God's people, it is a sin for us to stand by and do nothing.

> Anyone, then, who knows the good he ought to do and doesn't do it, sins.
>
> —James 4:17

We must research candidates to determine where they stand on issues. Also, we should find out who their supporters are. For example, if a candidate has the endorsement of those with perverted beliefs or lifestyles, we know he is not the right person to be given authority, no matter how nice looking or charming he is. And we can't judge candidates by polls or popular opinion, but by what they believe and stand for. Do they stand for righteousness, truth, justice, and mercy?

Let's not judge what they did thirty years ago, but what they have done recently. Candidates are only human and will make mistakes. But if they humble themselves and receive Christ as Lord, they can develop into a completely different person than thirty years before. If they made recent mistakes, what is their attitude concerning the error? Are they willing to admit the mistakes? Will they accept correction? What are their current beliefs?

With God's help, we can judge righteously in our families, in the Church, and in the political arena. Only then can we see revival in our nation. If no one is judged righteously and held accountable, we will continue our nation's moral decay. Our lack of discipline and correction will result in the destruction of our civilization.

Jesus said we could know a person by their fruit. Is their harvest good or bad, as shown by how a good tree produces good, and a corrupt tree gives little or none? We must use God's Word as the standard when we judge people or the affairs of our own lives. Without the Bible, people do what is right in their own eyes, as in Deuteronomy 12:8; 12:28 and Judges 21:25. Without the Word of God, Proverbs 14:12 tells us we have no discernment for right and wrong.

God, speaking through many men, taught us how we should live and what is good and acceptable in His sight. The Laws of Moses, such as the Ten Commandments, animal sacrifices, feasts and ordinances all pointed to Jesus. Teaching from prophets and apostles did also, says Luke 24:27. He is our Savior and mediates between God and man, according to Hebrews 9:14-15. There is no other name under heaven by which we can be saved, Acts 4:12 makes clear. Furthermore, the Laws of Moses, the prophets, the apostles and Jesus, Himself, all proclaim God's truth. They teach us right from wrong.

We know God loves a sinner but hates the sin. So we too, as disciples, are to love people but hate their sin. God loves us even in our sins. Moreover, without repentance and Jesus' cleansing blood, we can have no fellowship with God.

Other religions may have forms of godliness, but according to Hebrews 9:22, without the shedding of blood there is no remission for sin. Like it or not, this is one of the most important spiritual laws of the universe! God's Word, not man's opinion, is His standard by which we are to judge. When pastors and men of God call for our nation to repent and turn to righteousness, those who resist are resisting God's Word, by which we must daily live and eventually die. It leads us to eternal life. In Isaiah 40:8 and 1st John 2:17, we see the world will pass away and all its lusts, but God's Word will stand forever. God and His Word never change. So when we observe words or actions, we are to see them in the light of God's Word.

> Heaven and earth will pass away, but my words will never pass away.
> —Matthew 24:35

Man in his fallen state has the potential for good and evil. We have the potential to humble ourselves and admit we need a Savior, to overcome evil with good, to sit in the heavenly places with Christ, to walk in holiness as sons of God.

On the other hand, man has a potential to go to the lowest depths of sin, to become perverted in his thinking, to commit horrendous crimes, to fall into gross immorality. Any of us can go either direction; our decisions determine which one.

Only God's grace keeps us from falling into a perverted lifestyle. And since we have been given such mercy, we must judge others in mercy. We must realize only God's grace keeps us above depravity. Observe a homeless drug addict; we could easily live in their shoes, if not for God's grace. For this reason, we can love the depraved while at the same time hate their sin and our own.

Pray God will enable us to judge righteously in all the affairs of our lives.

Fruit Inspection

1. Why does God judge an individual? (Acts 16:31; Jeremiah 17:10)

   _____

2. What are some ways that we as Christians can judge a person's fruit? (Matthew 7:15-20)

   _____

3. Is it God's will for us to suffer with sin, sickness, and disease? Why or why not? (3 John 1:2)

   _____

4. Is it God's will for his people to be persecuted for righteousness sake?

   _____
   _____
   _____
   _____

   Why or why not? (Isaiah 54:15)

   _____
   _____
   _____
   _____

5. List some reasons why afflictions enter our lives.

   _____
   _____
   _____
   _____

   Does He use suffering to teach us spiritual lessons? (Psalm 119:67)

   _____
   _____
   _____
   _____

6. Our main purpose in this life is to produce good fruit. Do we bear fruit by trying to live as a good person or by obeying the Laws of Moses?

   _____
   _____
   _____

7. According to Jesus, how can we produce good fruit for the kingdom of God? (John 15:4-5)
   _____
   _____
   _____
   _____

   How does God purge us, in order for us to produce more fruit?
   _____
   _____
   _____
   _____

8. When God purges us, what does this prove? (Hebrews 12:6-7)
   _____
   _____
   _____
   _____

   What are some ways God purged you in the past?
   _____
   _____
   _____
   _____

   Did you grow spiritually through these experiences?
   _____
   _____
   _____
   _____

JUDGING THE FRUIT OF RIGHTEOUSNESS • 131

In what ways were you changed?
_____
_____
_____

9. What happens if we cease to bring a fruitful harvest? (John 15:6)
_____
_____
_____

10. Do you currently grow good fruit in your life?
_____
_____
_____

11. Give some examples of your fruit:
_____
_____
_____

   A. In your home
   _____
   _____
   _____

   B. In your school or place of employment
   _____
   _____

C. In your nation

12. How does Webster's Dictionary define "judge"?

13. In this sense of the word, are Christians to judge? (1 Corinthians 6:1-3)

14. The Apostle Paul says we, as Christians, are to judge ourselves. (1 Corinthians 11:31-32)

How do we judge ourselves?

JUDGING THE FRUIT OF RIGHTEOUSNESS • 133

15. If Christians will one day judge nations, what did Jesus mean when He instructed the disciples to "judge not"? (Luke 6:37)
   _____
   _____
   _____
   _____

16. What are examples of correct and incorrect ways for Christians to judge?
   _____
   _____
   _____
   _____

   A. At home
   _____
   _____
   _____
   _____

   B. At school or work
   _____
   _____
   _____
   _____

   C. In the nation
   _____
   _____
   _____
   _____

17. One way to judge ourselves is to know strong and weak points in our character. What are some of your strong points?

_____
_____
_____

What are your weak points?

_____
_____
_____

How can you improve in these areas?

_____
_____
_____

Chapter 4

CLEANSING AN UNHEALTHY BODY

The next area of judgment involves Christ's Church. How does God judge His Church? And how should we, as the body of Christ, judge one another? There is a difference between God's judgment of the Church and of the world. With the Church, He disciplines His own children.

> And you have forgotten that word of encouragement that addresses you as sons: "My son, do not make light of the Lord's discipline, and do not lose heart when he rebukes you, because the Lord disciplines those he loves, and he punishes everyone he accepts as a son." Endure hardship as discipline; God is treating you as sons. For what son is not disciplined by his father?
> —Hebrews 12:5-7

God will judge and correct His Church in this life quicker than He corrects the world, which will be judged in the life to come. For this reason, He gives plenty of time to repent. God has higher expectations for His family. His Bride is spared terrible judgments, which await the unrepentant, unbelieving. So God prepares His Church to walk as sons of God.

John the Baptist exposed the works of darkness in men's hearts. Jesus continued the Prophet John's work. But He provided further insight on forgiveness, love, and escape by God's power.

As mentioned in our previous chapter, God chastens us today with His Word. He speaks through it by His Holy Spirit's power. And since God writes His commandments on our hearts, we know when we disobey Him. Because of this indwelling helper, we are more aware of His commands than the world is. And as a good parent who has set rules, God won't allow us to sin without correction. If one continues in sin without correction, it proves they don't belong to God.

A four-year-old toddler won't be held as accountable as a teenager, or have the same expectations of him. A toddler won't be asked to carry out garbage or mow a lawn. They don't have as strict table manners, and they may be allowed immature behavior like pouting.

Similarly, one who is a babe in Christ will not be judged as strictly as a mature believer who has grown spiritually. God will have more patience toward a babe in Christ. But he will demand more from one who has been perfected by the Spirit of the Word.

Instructions on Discipline

God is longsuffering and will always give us plenty of opportunity to repent, and He gives us specific instructions on discipline within His Church. If a transgressor refuses to receive correction from Scripture, God will send a believer or preacher to correct him. If God's child still refuses to repent or change, He will allow discipline. If, having faced afflictions, a believer still refuses to listen; God will withdraw fellowship from him. We see this pattern of correction in Jesus' instructions on how to resolve conflict with a church member.

> If your brother sins against you, go and show him his fault, just between the two of you. If he listens to you, you have won your brother over. But if he will not listen, take one or two others along, so that "every matter may be established by the testimony of two or three witnesses." If he refuses to listen to them, tell it to the church; and if he refuses to listen even to the church, treat him as you would a pagan or a tax collector.
> —Matthew 18:15-17

Jesus gives an example of how we should correct our brothers. We aren't to tell everyone about an offense, stirring up strife. We are to go directly to a person who offended us and confront them. What is our motive? Is it to hurl our anger or nurse a grudge? Is it to condemn and prove we are right? Is it revenge? None of the above!

We confront one who has wronged us so he can see his error and repent. We attempt to correct him so he doesn't continue down a path of destruction, but will judge himself. This allows his soul to prosper. With this goal in mind, we must always correct with love and humility.

If a person still refuses to listen, Jesus said to take two or three witnesses and repeat the attempt, but don't look for someone to take your side. Rather, we are to find friends or Church elders with wisdom and knowledge of God. Our hope is a transgressor will respect mature believers and listen. Then they might recognize, admit their error, be willing to apologize, and change.

If confrontation with a small group doesn't solve the situation, our next step is to take the matter to Church leaders. This final attempt to save a brother from judgment is more public. The Bible tells us there will come a day when all things done, thought, or said in secret will be brought out for everyone to see. One day all of our unrepentant sins will be exposed.

So it's far better that our sins be exposed in this life than in the one to come, though both are embarrassing. The hope is always for a believer to feel convicted of his transgression and repent. It is better for us to be embarrassed and saved from God's judgment than to go down a path of destruction.

If we try all these steps and a person still refuses to repent, Jesus instructs us to treat him as a heathen and publican. So let's think, how were heathens and publicans of Jesus' day treated? For one, Jews refused to be in their company. Similarly, we are to cut off fellowship with those who profess to be Christians yet continue in sin. But we must remember to take action with a motive of love, not with anger or to revenge, which is not easy. For the fallen person's own well being, we are commanded to remove fellowship.

Like our Creator, we must hate sin, because it leads to death and destruction. However, we must also love a person who falls into sin and want to see them return to God. So we withhold fellowship, in the hope they will realize their mistake, like the prodigal son. All the while we are told to pray for them, while we wait for their heart to soften and mind to agree. Only then can an errant person receive correction.

Keep in mind, Jesus does not talk about people who unwillingly make mistakes—those who walk in ignorance. Jesus addresses people who clearly know they are doing wrong yet stubbornly persist anyway, with no desire to change! He warns us not to hold God's commandments in contempt. If one admits his faults, wants to change, asks for prayer, or seeks counsel, we are to encourage and take care of him, as a good shepherd cares for his sheep.

All of us in the body of Christ have some responsibility of discipline within the church. Individual church members should hold one another accountable in their own personal relationships and sphere of influence. A Sunday school teacher can be a source of accountability to his or her class. Our church has men's and women's fellowships in which we are required to get an accountability partner to encourage, confide in, and hold one another accountable.

Some problems may arise that are beyond what a church member feels capable or comfortable dealing with. In these cases, the problem should be referred to the church leaders. Those church leaders who are called and anointed by God will have special grace, training, and preparation to deal with various situations that may require discipline.

Occasionally, a situation arises in which the pastor should step forward and confront the problem, whether through prayer, counseling, or publicly addressing the congregation, applying the appropriate discipline. However, when addressing the congregation publicly, the pastor should try to avoid mentioning specific names, or publicly embarrassing anyone. Although pastors should not be dictators, God has given church leaders positions of authority, which should be respected by the congregation. We are all ultimately accountable to God.

Like a father disciplines his children, we are to always discipline in love. Church authorities can discipline God's sheep in a loving, but firm way. Like parents, pastors should hold their members accountable, while assuring them of acceptance and unconditional love. While purging eliminates impurities, discipline teaches us obedience. Both have the goal of bearing more good fruit for the kingdom of God.

So what are we to do with a brother who continues in sin, even though he claims to know Christ? Do we overlook his unwillingness to repent and pretend everything is well? Are we to ask him to dinner occasionally, simply for fun, but never mention spiritual subjects so we don't offend him? Will he perhaps eventually like us so much, he will want to repent?

Do we stalk him and try to persuade a change? Maybe we should knock on his door. If he refuses to answer, we can call his cell phone. If he hangs up, should we find out where he works and visit him at the office? We can search for him at the bars where he meets dates. Then we could announce in front of all his friends what a wicked person he is and how he's going to hell if he doesn't change.

The answer, according to the Scriptures, lies in none of these ideas. We can pray and trust in the Holy Spirit to deal with his heart. We can also discipline through persuasion and corrective counseling. If he still refuses to listen to correction, Paul says to avoid close fellowship with him as a last resort. The Bible's way of discipline is to withdraw fellowship and treat him as one who has never known Christ.

Paul's Divine Correction

The Apostle Paul taught and practiced these teachings of Jesus concerning discipline in the Church. Confronting others over sin requires that we be sensitive to the leading of the Holy Spirit. Each problem involving church discipline is unique with unique people. We must rely on the Holy Spirit to show us the proper timing and approach. Usually, we should give the Holy Spirit time to deal with the errant person and just intercede in prayer on their behalf. The Holy Spirit may lead us differently, depending on the individual and the circumstance.

The apostles mentioned some of the sins which required church discipline. Those mentioned in 1 Corinthians 5:9-11 include adultery, fornication, covetousness, extortion, idolatry, and drunkenness. Paul also instructed the church to avoid those who are constantly angry and sow strife. In addition, he instructed us to avoid those who refuse to work, but instead, meddle in others' affairs, creating gossip and strife. We should keep in mind that all of us have sinned. When confronting others, we must guard ourselves against arrogance, harshness, and hypocrisy.

However, if one continues to refuse correction, we should take the appropriate disciplinary measures. We are to break fellowship with those who call themselves Christians, yet who continue in evil. This is not to be from arrogance or self-righteousness, but to cause the person to feel shame, so they will return to our fellowship and our Father, like the prodigal son. Unless they change, the Word of God says their path of sin will lead to death. Romans 8:6 says to be carnal minded leads to death. Romans 6:23 is also clear: the wages of sin is death.

> If anyone does not obey our instruction in this letter, take special note of him. Do not associate with him, in order that he may feel ashamed. Yet do not regard him as an enemy, but warn him as a brother.
> —2 Thessalonians 3:14-15

Notice this verse restates to count the person under discipline as a brother or sister, not as an enemy. Although we part company with them, we're to always love them; they remain our family in the Lord. If they repent and ask forgiveness, the Church should always welcome them back with open arms, for they were lost and now are found. They were dead and are alive again. When a backslider returns to God, it is a great time of rejoicing!

Paul says if a man does not obey the Scriptures, note that man. The Darby translation says to mark that man and have no company with him. Why? The answer lies in the following historical episode.

Sin in the Camp

In the church at Corinth, a man was committing adultery with his father's wife. Paul doesn't go into details about the relationship. It could have been incest, or maybe it was his stepmother. Possibly, his father had died while they lived together. It's conceivable they attended church together and sat by one another.

Paul implies in his letter they did not attempt to hide their sin. Perhaps this man donated large financial contributions to the church. Maybe as a community leader, he did charitable works. For some reason, the church of Corinth refused to confront him about his adulterous affair. But in his first letter to the Corinthian church, Paul directly addressed the situation:

> It is actually reported that there is sexual immorality among you, and of a kind that does not occur even among pagans: A man has his father's wife. And you are proud! Shouldn't you rather have been filled with grief and have put out of your fellowship the man who did this?
> —1 Corinthians 5:1-2

Why did Paul feel it necessary to confront this believer? Did he feel superior to those who had fallen into sin? Was he self-righteous? Did Paul try to humiliate this couple? Was he a judgmental, legalistic Pharisee? No. Paul was constrained by love to take this action.

He knew if nothing was done, this couple living in sin would eventually lose their souls. So Paul knew it was better for them to be confronted now than to fall away from God, crucifying Christ afresh, as it says in Hebrews 6:4-6. Paul loved them so much he risked a confrontation. Paul judged the situation and took action!

> Even though I am not physically present, I am with you in spirit. And I have already passed judgment on the one who did this, just as if I were present. When you are assembled in the name of our Lord Jesus and I am with you in spirit, and the power of our Lord Jesus is present, hand this man over to Satan, so that the sinful nature may be destroyed and his spirit saved on the day of the Lord.
> —1 Corinthians 5:3-5

Paul didn't simply write a nice letter, but aware of the authority Christ had given him as an apostle, he bravely dealt with spiritual issues. He was willing to allow Satan to destroy the flesh of this couple so their spirits could be saved. And he addressed this situation to God in prayer. Paul learned from Jesus' teachings it is better to pluck out an eye and go to heaven than to end up in hell with good eyesight!

Paul also operated on the revelation that he had decided to turn this couple over to Satan for destruction of their flesh. As a last resort, Paul planned to give them over to afflictions and hope it led them to repentance. This may seem like witchcraft, except Paul was led by the Holy Spirit and motivated by love. But not all believers walk in this type of authority. Only those who humble themselves to walk in love and maturity can be entrusted with such authority, only with divine power.

There is a happy ending to this story. In Paul's second letter to the Corinthians, we find this couple, as well as the whole church, repented with godly sorrow and with a holy zeal. Paul admonished the believers to abstain from all filthiness of the flesh, perfecting holiness and the fear of God. He then proceeds to commend them for a willingness to heed his warning:

> …and not only by his coming but also by the comfort you had given him. He told us about your longing for me, your deep

sorrow, your ardent concern for me, so that my joy was greater than ever. Even if I caused you sorrow by my letter, I do not regret it. Though I did regret it—I see that my letter hurt you, but only for a little while—yet now I am happy, not because you were made sorry, but because your sorrow led you to repentance. For you became sorrowful as God intended and so were not harmed in any way by us. Godly sorrow brings repentance that leads to salvation and leaves no regret, but worldly sorrow brings death. See what this godly sorrow has produced in you: what earnestness, what eagerness to clear yourselves, what indignation, what alarm, what longing, what concern, what readiness to see justice done. At every point you have proved yourselves to be innocent in this matter.

—2 Corinthians 7:7-11

We find Paul rejoicing at their desire to please God. His first letter led to repentance after godly sorrow. But there is another kind of sorrow: worldly sorrow, without hope, which leads to death. But godly sorrow leads to repentance by faith. Worldly sorrow leads to sin consciousness. Those who have only worldly sorrow are sorry for their consequences. However, they have no desire to change nor the faith to change. Godly sorrow leads to God consciousness. Godly sorrow will lead to change because of faith in Jesus, the One who gives power to change.

The Corinthian church went to great lengths to make things right. Upon receiving Paul's letter, they took swift action to correct the problem. As a result, this couple repented; Paul forgave them, and everyone welcomed them back into the fellowship of believers.

What might have happened if Paul had let this situation slide, as much of the church does today? Had their sin continued unabated, it could have resulted in much sorrow and eventually led to death. Because Paul took action, the Corinthian church was spared judgment.

Purge Old Leaven

> Your boasting is not good. Don't you know that a little yeast works through the whole batch of dough? Get rid of the old yeast that you may be a new batch without yeast—as you really are. For Christ, our Passover lamb, has been sacrificed.
> —1 Corinthians 5:6-7

It was crucial for Paul to discipline the Corinthians. If this situation was not corrected, sin could have spread throughout their church like a carnivorous cancer. But Paul acted, quick and decisive, to remove it from the body of Christ. This explains why Paul also instructed the Thessalonians to mark any man who does not obey God's commandments.

Failure of discipline in the Church results in lasciviousness. Truth is suppressed, which allows erroneous teaching to spread. Left unchecked, sins will spread, and any church will become like the world, no longer able to discern good from evil.

We have failed in this generation to hold one another accountable for our actions. We have forgotten how to confront and discipline. Perhaps in the past it was done with arrogance and self-righteousness rather than love. Consequently, many churches today are full of sin, wickedness, and corruption. Sin's leaven has spread; it's hard to separate our actions from the world's.

A major difference between the early church and our modern ones is we fail to purge sin's leaven. Therefore, many who attend church head down a road of sorrow, destruction, and death. Even church leaders indulge in adultery, homosexuality, child molestation, and all manner of wickedness.

So, how do we purge evil? Prayer is the most effective way. We must also, with the Holy Spirit's guidance, confront those who continue to live in sin. If we truly love them, we will confront them. If we care about their souls, we will risk loss of relationship.

> I have written you in my letter not to associate with sexually immoral people—not at all meaning the people of this world who are immoral, or the greedy and swindlers, or idolaters. In that case you would have to leave this world. But now I am writing you that you must not associate with anyone who calls himself a brother but is sexually immoral or greedy, an idolater or a slanderer, a drunkard or a swindler. With such a man do not even eat.
> —1 Corinthians 5:9-11

We are told only to have limited fellowship with those who are not born again, worldly unbelievers. Of course we work with and see them at public places and do business together. Yet while we are commanded not be close friends, we are also to have contact, to be salt and light, as Mark 2:15-17 tells us.

Patience is a key factor with people who are new in the body of Christ. They need time for God to mature them from new babes. So we must not judge them harshly but remember how God brought us from the depths of darkness, as we're reminded in Galatians 6:1. Like it takes time for a little tree to grow to a mighty oak, it will take time for new believers to grow spiritually. All God asks for, as 1 Peter 2:2-3 says, is a humble, willing heart.

On the other hand, we are to avoid those who call themselves Christians, yet deliberately continue their works of the flesh. People do have plenty of time to repent and grow in the knowledge of God, yet many refuse. This includes people who once knew God's truths yet returned to live like an unbeliever.

Paul says we are not even to have a meal together, in 1 Corinthians 5:11. We avoid them as a last resort, only after trying every means of reasonable persuasion mentioned by Jesus in Matthew 18:15-17. We can only pursue them in prayer, to try to win them back to God, but we are not to fellowship. They can't take our time away from others willing to listen and repent. God will never give up on a person, but at the same time, He will not violate their free will or force their choices.

We separate from rebellious people who call themselves Christians not because we are unkind or cruel, but to awaken their spiritual sense. Some people continue in immorality and are deceived. Like nonbelievers, the god of this world blinds their eyes and minds. So we take drastic action in hope they will see the truth. And when we refuse fellowship, tell them why, so they can see their destructive path. Love takes risks, even if it costs friendships.

> In the name of the Lord Jesus Christ, we command you, brothers, to keep away from every brother who is idle and does not live according to the teaching you received from us.
> —2 Thessalonians 3:6

Dare I Risk Confrontation?

God revealed this revelation to confront sin to me as a young man in my late twenties. I had a number of dear friends who became enticed into sin. Yet they still continued to attend church, thinking everything was okay, and called themselves Christians. But the sin continued. I struggled with this for weeks. I prayed. I hoped they might change. Finally, after months and in some cases years, I confronted each person. Very few responded with humility or kindness. Most of them felt offended.

It may cost us to stand for righteousness and confront someone in love. I was accused of being legalistic, judgmental, and self-righteous. So I examined my motives to see if this was true. My choice to confront these friends resulted in broken fellowship with many of them, and I often wondered if I had done the right thing. For a long time I missed their friendship, and I felt grieved.

Later, after I received a fuller revelation and understanding about divine correction, I realized confrontation was indeed necessary. Most of these friends approached me weeks or months later to apologize and thank me. Sadly, I've never heard from others. Still, I have peace. I know their blood will *not* be on my hands, as it says in Ezekiel 33:6. And I know God has not given up on them, either. Perhaps He will send other people across their path, who will bring them back home, into His loving arms.

Discipline of Teachers and Ministers

Paul also instructs us on how to discipline teachers and ministers within the Church. Paul told Timothy to withdraw himself from teachers who stir up strife and who twist truth.

> If anyone teaches false doctrines and does not agree to the sound instruction of our Lord Jesus Christ and to godly teaching, he is conceited and understands nothing. He has an unhealthy interest in controversies and quarrels about words that result in envy, strife, malicious talk, evil suspicions and constant friction between men of corrupt mind, who have been robbed of the truth and who think that godliness is a means to financial gain.
> —I Timothy 6:3-5

Paul addresses Timothy about teachers who are in churches for selfish gain. They are proud and in continual strife, refusing correction. They criticize others who teach holiness and repentance. They judge the poor harshly and think only gain is godly. But it's clear; churches are to discipline teachers, as well as any other believer.

How do we do that? We withdraw from them. We stop attending their meetings and cease to support their ministries. But let me reiterate, we are not to be cruel, but always have a goal to bring these teachers back into the truth of Jesus Christ.

Discipline within a Family

The same principles hold true for discipline within a family. Sometimes parents can never admit their children are at fault. While it is an established truth that love defends, real love does not compromise truth. Our children cannot be helped if they are not held accountable. Their behavior will only get worse!

I've known parents who never confront or discipline their children—ever! Then, when a child gets into trouble at school, they say it's always the teacher's fault. When they get into fights, it's always the other child's fault.

These parents may also allow their children to be the head of the house. Eventually, their children may get into alcohol, drugs, or sexual promiscuity. But instead of confronting them, some parents unbelievably give the youths money to get them out of the house, where they continue their destructive behavior. Instead of taking a stand against illicit sex, they may give their children condoms for "protection."

And parents can have similar problems with alcohol and sex, themselves. Maybe they, too, were never confronted or disciplined as children. So a continual cycle of lawlessness and destruction races from one generation to another. A few children end up in jail, and their parents bail them out of trouble.

A child or young adult may never feel accountable to anyone because they know Mom or Dad will always rescue them. While these parents think they give their children unconditional love, they never realize unconditional love involves discipline and guidance too. It never dawns on them that it is better to cut off your hand and enter into heaven with a missing hand, than to be cast into hell with both hands; it is better to be judged in this life than in the life to come. If they understood this revelation, they would take action to stop their children's destructive behavior!

So, what actions should be taken to prevent and stop destructive behavior? Many books are available on how to raise children. However, I will briefly list a few steps we can take to prevent destructive behavior.

First, we are to get on our knees and pray for our children. Don't wait until they are in prison to do it, but pray for them in their mother's womb. Read and confess God's Word over them—early!

Second, teach children the Word of God at home. Teach them right from wrong from God's viewpoint. Our homes should be a classroom about God, as well as Sunday school.

> These commandments that I give you today are to be upon your hearts. Impress them on your children. Talk about them when you sit at home and when you walk along the road, when you lie down and when you get up.
> —Deuteronomy 6:6-7

Third, don't be concerned if your children call you preachy. If they ask you to quit preaching, remind them you are obeying God. But make sure you don't only criticize, but encourage them as well, teaching in love.

Are we to obey God or our children? Who is Lord of our house, anyway? We aren't only to teach God's Word, but we are to set good examples as parents. However, don't allow accusations from your children to keep you from teaching.

Fourth, no one is perfect, and we, as parents, will make mistakes. If our children see us sin, we must be willing to admit our mistakes, which is repentance, and ask forgiveness from them. Then, they must see us change. They should see that we, as adults, discipline ourselves. This will make our children more willing to receive correction, because they see it is possible to do.

Fifth, we must discipline. Our children must realize when their behavior is unacceptable. While we assure them of our love, we are commanded to take action, to help remove the leaven of rebellion in their hearts. There are many Christian books on how to discipline. Find one and study it, for everyone's sake.

Finally, demonstrate love. They need to know we will always support them. At the same time, it needs to be clear they will be held accountable for all destructive behavior. Spend time with them. Listen. Play games. Have fun; they are gifts from God.

Do We Really Want Revival?

Occasionally, the Holy Spirit will step in to discipline church members, handing them over to Satan for the destruction of the flesh. Such was the case with Ananias and Sapphira. This is their sad story:

Barnabas, who later traveled with the Apostle Paul, sold a piece of land and brought the money as an offering to the apostles. He didn't have to, but he did it as a symbol of total surrender to Christ, and God honored his sincere heart. God promoted Barnabas and gave him wisdom and authority. Remember, God always knows the innermost thoughts and intentions of our hearts and minds.

Having seen how Barnabas was promoted, Ananias and Sapphira decided to achieve the same effect. But they were not giving to God, but to impress people, to be seen and admired by others. Their gift wasn't an act of worship, but an act of selfishness! They jockeyed for power and status within the Church body by also selling land and giving it to the church. But they lied and said it was the entire sum, while they brought only part of the money and laid it at the apostles' feet.

> Then Peter said, "Ananias, how is it that Satan has so filled your heart that you have lied to the Holy Spirit and have kept for yourself some of the money you received for the land? Didn't it belong to you before it was sold? And after it was sold, wasn't

the money at your disposal? What made you think of doing such a thing? You have not lied to men but to God." When Ananias heard this, he fell down and died. And great fear seized all who heard what had happened.

—Acts 5:3-5

Ananias' wife, Sapphira, later came into the church, unaware that her husband had died for his lie. She also changed the facts she told the apostles. An instant later she also died. The Holy Spirit took it personally. When we offend or rebel against leaders God has placed over our church, we don't rebel against men.

"You have not lied unto men, but unto God," Peter said.

"How could God be so cruel?" we might ask.

Then we have to remember He sees things from a different perspective than we do. And to be judged in this life is far better than to lose our soul. So this couple's death was an act of God's mercy. His intervention destroyed their bodies, but may have saved their souls. Ananias and Sapphira died instantly. Their spirits left their bodies in a moment of time, so they did not suffer.

God was moving in their area in a great revival. The Church had gained momentum and God's Word spread in mighty power. Many people repented, surrendering to the Lordship of Jesus Christ. Had God allowed Ananias and Sapphira to get by with this lie, the leaven of sin might have spread throughout the Church. It could have doused the flames of revival. For the sake of the entire Church, swift judgment had to be the consequence for their lies.

Many people today covet high status and position within their church. They play church politics and try to promote themselves, for admiration from people. They flatter those in authority, attempting to gain status. Yet, even if they achieve power among men, they will have no power with God. Like Ananias and Sapphira, some people covet power to the extent they will deceive to obtain it. What they don't realize is God knows their acts, thoughts, and intentions.

If churches today operated in the same power as the early church in the book of Acts, judgment would be swift. God waits for us to wash our minds and actions with His Word before He can bring us to the glorious state of maturity He desires. If the Church truly means business with God today, it is time we examine our individual hearts and weep before His Holy Altar.

Many people pray for revival. But do we really realize what accompanies it? Revival includes the presence of God Almighty. Granted, there is a great outpouring of His love. But at the same time, His judgment is also outpoured. Are those who pray for revival aware of this fact? Remember, God's judgment is always motivated by love.

HOLINESS VS. PROSPERITY

There have been conflicts in churches between these two lines of thought. Those who are called to preach judgment and holiness criticize the prosperity message, calling it worldly and self-centered. The prosperity camp criticizes those who teach judgment as negative, doomsday preachers, bound by the law. The truth is both messages are needed in the body of Christ. We should embrace the whole council of God.

> Therefore let us leave the elementary teachings about Christ and go on to maturity, not laying again the foundation of repentance from acts that lead to death, and of faith in God, instruction about baptisms, the laying on of hands, the resurrection of the dead, and eternal judgment.
> —Hebrews 6:1-2

We aren't allowed to pick and choose parts of God's Word we like or enjoy hearing and throw out the rest. A healthy fear of the Lord can create in us a desire to halt sinful patterns and receive

Jesus as our Lord. Faith enables us to become sons of God, to live His Word and obey His commandments. Love establishes our relationship. Without a message of judgment, why should the wicked repent? Without the message of faith, there is no power to obey. And with no message of love, we never know mercy and forgiveness.

If people aren't taught God's commandments, how can they realize we all fall short of God's glory? How can they feel a need for a Savior? Since many of our generation today have not been taught integrity, honor, honesty, self-control, and the fruit of righteousness, they are deceived into believing a lie that there is no God, or they do not need Him.

"I'm not so bad. I'm not as bad as most people. I'm all right with God. I don't need Christ," they say.

The truth is we don't come close to living perfectly. Men considered holy, like Mohammad or Buddha, fell far short of God's standards. No one can live for God without Christ. Even the apostles needed to walk in humility, with an attitude of repentance.

Repentance is, in reality, a message of prosperity, implied throughout God's Word. If we repent and obey His commandments, we will prosper. This doesn't mean we won't miss the mark sometimes. It does not imply we will never suffer or be persecuted. Rather, it implies God will give us the grace to endure—anything.

Prosperity in God's kingdom means we will have our *needs* totally met. Our most important needs are righteousness, peace, joy, love, and contentment. God gives different gifts to believers to emphasize different doctrines. Some are called to preach faith, others teach healing or repentance or judgment. A pastor is responsible for his sheep to get a well-balanced diet of the Word.

Let me make it clear, I am not against the prosperity message. One reason the Holy Spirit sent me to Tulsa, Oklahoma, is because I desperately needed to hear this message of faith. I thank God for men who preach faith and prosperity. They have fulfilled their calling, covering our nation with the message. Yet, this message is desperately needed, and there is still much to be taught.

On the other hand, repentance and judgment are not preached enough in our nation. One reason is because these messages bring much persecution. They are politically incorrect. Those who do are labeled as intolerant, negative, judgmental, and condemning. But we must understand it is good to teach right from wrong.

Indeed, if we fail to address evil in our society, our nation is doomed to destruction. If the rebellious only hear about God's love, without His justice, they will continue down the road of death and influence others to do the same. There is a vast difference between condemnation and the convicting power of the Holy Spirit. Unfortunately, there are others called to preach on judgment and repentance, but they refuse. They fear of men more than God.

"How can I preach holiness when I, myself, fall so short?" they say.

Because you make an occasional mistake, it doesn't mean you cannot take a stand to label right and wrong as good and evil. But we should take a stand in love, not from arrogance. There are areas in everyone's life where we fall short. But when we stand for what is right, God gives a special grace to overcome in our weaknesses.

When we are inspired by the Holy Spirit of God, words we speak and write are not our own. A person God uses as His spokesman will have often attained a degree of personal victory by having spent time with the Father. However, he won't be perfect because he is only human.

For example, we see righteousness preached in David's psalms, yet he made a terrible mistake with Bathsheba. How can David write beautiful psalms of truth yet commit such a flagrant sin? Because he was inspired by the Spirit of God! The words were not his own, but God's. David was a man after God's own heart—not perfect—but with a heart for God. He loved to walk with God.

Unfortunately, cares and pressures of a kingdom choked David's time. Soon, he spent less time with God and became less aware of His presence. He gradually had fewer thoughts toward God and more of the world and problems of ruling a nation. Then fiery darts of our enemy began to penetrate David's mind. As a result, he didn't resist temptation.

But we must remember David lived under the old covenant. He didn't have the Holy Spirit's power like we can have today. Also, we must keep in mind that David did not continue to sin. As a matter of fact, this was unusual for him. He repented and never made the same mistake again.

Our eyes are to be fixed on Jesus, not on men. The apostles and prophets weren't perfect, yet they denounced sins and idols of their day. The Church, as a whole, has failed to boldly confront sin. As a result of this neglect, our nation has fallen into its present condition of lawlessness.

Our Itching Ears

Those who only receive a message of prosperity and love, but exclude the rest of God's council, face a danger of falling into lasciviousness. They may claim to follow our Messiah, but no one could ever tell by their lifestyle, only wanting to hear about blessings. Self-centered, they always think about what God will give them, rather than what they can do for Him and for others.

Then they get offended when the Holy Spirit disciplines. Seeking people's praise, they quickly fall away when persecution comes. They refuse to repent, unwilling to change! Any attempts by a pastor or fellow believers to correct them are met with accusations of being judgmental, even though correction is done in love.

These people always quote the first part of Romans 8:1, "There is therefore now no condemnation to them which are in Christ Jesus." But they fail to put this partial quotation within the full context of the scriptures and never finish the verse: "Who walk not after the flesh, but after the Spirit." This clearly implies, if we walk after the flesh, there will be condemnation.

Does God condemn them? No, they condemn themselves by choosing to walk after the flesh rather than the Spirit. Paul continues to expound on the difference between carnal minded and spiritually minded.

> The mind of sinful man is death, but the mind controlled by the Spirit is life and peace.
> —Romans 8:6

So we see, those who continue to be carnal minded and walk after the flesh will be judged. If they refuse to repent, their carnality will result in death. However, God will give plenty of time to repent, especially to those who only recently were born again. In churches that reject the message of repentance we find fornication, homosexuality, dishonesty, gossip, and other works of darkness. And if a pastor refuses to address these issues of evil, their church continues exactly like Satan's world.

We, God's Church of this generation, must reverence God and respect His Word. The time has come for us in Europe and America to live and believe God's truth. True reverence for God results in our obedience. God's Word says, if one claims to respect God yet continues to disobey His commandments, that person is deceived.

> The man who says, "I know him," but does not do what he commands is a liar, and the truth is not in him.
> —1 John 2:4

- If we respect God's Word, we will study it.
- Not only will we meditate on it, but also obey it by faith.

- If God says we rob Him when we withhold tithes and offerings, then as Malachi 3:8 says, we can begin giving to God—joyfully!
- When God says He hates adultery and divorce, we should hate it too! Verses to note are Psalm 45:7, Jeremiah 29:23, Malachi 2:16.
- When God calls homosexuality an abomination or detestable, as in Leviticus 18:22, we should also see it as filthy.
- He says in His Word we are not to murmur, grumble, or complain against Him, which Numbers 14:27-29 shows, but we can obtain His promises by giving thanks.
- We need to quit making excuses and obey the Spirit's voice!

God is the same. He never changes. Hebrews 13:8 reminds us: "Jesus Christ the same yesterday, today, and forever." If He said adultery is worthy of death in ancient times, it's worthy of death today too, in His eyes. Leviticus 20:10 tells us this. God hates adultery and sodomy as much today as in Moses' generation. So we ask, why are we not put to death today for such sins? It is only because of Jesus' blood. The new covenant does not change God's opinion about such sins. He still despises evil.

But why does God hate adultery so much? Because it destroys families. It hurts many people, especially children. I've known several persons abandoned by a spouse. Every one attests it causes more sorrow than losing a spouse through physical death. Some confess the pain is almost unbearable.

Adultery also breaks trust. A marriage covenant is more than an ordinary business contract; it's also holy commitment, holy unto the Lord. It represents a commitment to God, a bond of lives; two become one flesh. Marriage involves abandoning ourselves to serve one another for a lifetime. Those who choose marriage unite in hopes, dreams, and their destiny of God. Marriage contains a special, unique bond, unlike any other relationship.

The Apostle Paul likens marriage to the relationship of Christ and His Church. Jesus told parables which also illustrated this. In the old covenant, God considered His relationship with Israel like a marriage, yet Israel forsook the Lord for idols. God accused Israel of acting like a harlot with other lovers in Hosea 2:5-2:13.

God knows the hurt and pain of rejection. He knows how it feels to give someone your all, only to be betrayed. Christ was rejected and forsaken. Sin cost God the death of His only Son. In God's opinion, those who cause such pain are worthy of death.

The new covenant makes it possible for our sins to be removed because Jesus took judgment upon Himself—a high price to pay! This is the glorious Gospel of salvation. His great sacrifice is why we will worship Him forever in a New Jerusalem. We owe it all to the Lamb of God.

Nevertheless, for our sins to be removed we need to repent and be willing to change. Many people miss this truth in churches today; they are deceived. They claim to know Christ yet have refused to repent of their sins. This explains why there are homosexual priests in some denominations. A person whose beliefs are in direct contradiction to God's Word should not be in Church leadership.

Explosion of Freedom and Disrespect

A great charismatic renewal began in the 1960s. Freedom of expression exploded in churches, especially among the youth. A few denominations allowed the Holy Spirit an explosion of freedom. However, Satan attempted to counteract this movement; he sowed seeds of disrespect, deception, and rebellion toward God's commandments.

To avoid judgment today, we need to return to a deep reverence for God, who never changes. If He brought judgment upon His early church, He will bring judgment today. When He gives us a commandment, we must not consider it a suggestion.

When I was a child in a Baptist church during the 1960s and '70s, there were no rock bands, no video games, and little entertainment. All we had was the pure milk of God's Word. It's not necessarily wrong to provide kids with entertainment at church; it can draw youths who wouldn't attend otherwise. Everyone needs entertainment and relaxation, but we need to keep it in its right perspective.

Our technological revolution has ushered in incredible prosperity for mankind. At the same time, it gives Christians new and dangerous temptations. Technology speeds our lifestyle, causing many of our generation, especially young people, to be more prone to boredom and discontentment, which can lead to evil, as shown in Philippians 4:11.

For this reason, many young people consider simple Bible reading and study boring. But, for them to grow in the knowledge of righteousness, most time at church should be spent learning the Word of God. And it requires discipline, which many of our day look on with disdain.

Entertainment for a short period will allow young people to unwind and expend their bottled-up energy. But if there is no Bible preaching, under the anointing and Holy Spirit's power, then a church provides nothing more for its youth than shallow entertainment. This leads to unfruitful evil and works of the flesh, and makes churches no different than the world. Maybe more youths attend churches today for the technology. But there is also more of our world in the Church, which causes youth to not know right from wrong.

Perhaps one reason many churches place such emphasis on entertainment is because they have never experienced a true manifestation of God's presence. Smith Wigglesworth, known to many as the Apostle of Faith, knew excitement from God's manifested presence.

> There is something in the Pentecostal work that is different than anything else in the world. Somehow, in Pentecost you know that God is a reality. Whenever the Holy Spirit has right-of-way, the gifts of the spirit will be in manifestation. Where these gifts are never in manifestation, I question whether He is present. Pentecostal people are spoiled for anything other than Pentecostal meetings. We want none of the entertainments that other churches are offering. When God comes in, He entertains us Himself. The King of Kings and Lord of Lords entertains us! Oh, it is wonderful.[1]

Some may say, "We live in a different generation. Times have changed." But according to the Bible in Hebrews 13:8, Jesus is the same yesterday, today, and forever. God has not changed, and if His Word is taught in the power of His Holy Spirit, young people will come.

Let's look at Jesus' ministry. Did He provide entertainment to draw people? No, He only preached the kingdom of God. At one point in His ministry, many people couldn't receive what He taught, so they stopped following Him. In the same way, a few young people will quit attending church if the Bible is taught without compromise. But what is worse, a few offended youth because of truth, or sin's leaven corrupting a church?

Based on the Word of God, it is better to train and discipline our young people than for them to lose their souls, so I'd rather be "preachy" than hip and cool. It's better for our youth to be bored yet cleaned by God's Word than entertained and on their way to hell. I'm not talking about physical training, but discipline from the Scriptures, through the Holy Spirit's power. We also discipline children spiritually, through prayer, like Paul and the church at Corinth.

Did Jesus panic and look for entertainment to bring the crowds back? Of course not. Instead, in John 6:67 He asked the people remaining, "Will you also leave?" Jesus was not concerned with popularity, but only with doing His Father's will. He wasn't concerned with men's opinions, but with teaching God's truth. When people refused to hear what He taught, He wasn't fretful or anxious.

Jesus didn't call a disciples' meeting and say, "Okay boys, attendance is down. Let's brainstorm ways to increase our audience. I want someone to take a seminar, and let's bring in the famous rock band, 'Dirty, Ugly Disciples.' Let's get a mortgage and build a gymnasium. And I will stop preaching correction and preach only love and prosperity."

By all means, we need to demonstrate God's love to our youth, but it involves discipline as well as kindness. We can't compromise God's truth for man's praise. If we preach truth, a few will always be offended, no matter how kind we are. So let's simply look to Jesus as our example.

The holy, spotless Lamb of God preached a holy, spotless message of truth. Before He sent His disciples to preach His Gospel, He had something to say about those who refused to receive His message of truth:

> If people do not welcome you, shake the dust off your feet when you leave their town, as a testimony against them.
> —Luke 9:5

Did Jesus tell them to beg and plead with the city to accept Christ? Did He say to brainstorm ways to draw people to His meetings? Did He chase people on the street to gain an audience? Never. His message of truth and demonstration of power were enough to draw people. He didn't have to pursue people; they sought Him. He didn't entice them with gimmicks or promotions. He didn't force His message on anyone unwilling to receive it. The power of prayer and God's anointing drew the crowds.

I experienced revivals at Baptist churches, from my youth through college. Each revival consisted, not of fads or entertainment, but the pure Word of God with the power of the Holy Spirit. No gimmicks brought them to church, but a genuine urging from the Holy Spirit.

God will do new things among his people, but it won't be shallow entertainment; His Holy Spirit will cause it. God birthed new worship during the Jesus Movement, not shallow entertainment. Anointed songs forever changed the lives of young people present. When God moves, they come to the altar in repentance. They surrender their lives wholly to the Lord and are never the same again.

Who Will Go for Me?

God will raise up preachers who will warn of judgments to come upon the earth. When they denounce sin and call for repentance, they may be persecuted and misunderstood. Many people will accuse them of intolerance and cruelty. Yet they will be constrained to preach this message, by the love of God and a hatred for evil. When they observe people heading down the broad road that leads to destruction, love and righteous anger stirs them to action. As they receive a revelation of coming terrors, God's love will not allow them to keep silent.

> Son of man, I have made you a watchman for the house of Israel; so hear the word I speak and give them warning from me. When I say to the wicked, "O wicked man, you will surely die," and you do not speak out to dissuade him from his ways, that wicked man will die for his sin, and I will hold you accountable for his blood. But if you do warn the wicked man to turn from his ways and he does not do so, he will die for his sin, but you will have saved yourself.
> —Ezekiel 33:7-9

During the 1980s and 1990s, a very small remnant of preachers admonished the United States to repent and turn to God, much as Ezekiel did Judah. At this time the church was too engulfed with the idea of material prosperity to even think of such a concept as repentance and judgment. Those who preached repentance were labeled as negative, doomsday preachers. During this time, my spirit was deeply grieved over my own failures, as well as all of the wickedness in America. Having studied the Bible extensively, I knew that our nation was ripe for judgment.

Yet after many years had passed in the 1990s, America's material prosperity continued to increase. I began to have my doubts. Perhaps I had been a bit pessimistic. After all, God wouldn't allow some catastrophe to strike our nation. There are still some God-fearing saints who live here. However, the Holy Spirit continued to bring into mind what Jesus said in Luke 12:48, "From everyone who has been given much, much will be demanded; and from the one who has been entrusted with much, much more will be asked." He reassured me that if America didn't change, judgment would surely come to pass. As a matter of fact, it had already begun in the form of rampant crime and violence. But it would take judgment on a wider scale to catch the attention of our nation. The delay was only because of God's great love and mercy: He is not willing any should perish, but all should come to eternal life. So years passed and no judgment came on a massive scale, even though our nation continued down a road of lawlessness.

When catastrophes did occur across the earth during the first decade of the 21st century, the church came together in unity and poured out God's love to the victims. We the church must preach repentance and warn of judgment, while at the same time demonstrate God's love. We must be well-balanced in teaching the doctrines of Christ.

Hard Taskmasters

Let's look at the opposite response. There are those who receive a message of judgment yet refuse the message of faith and love. These believers become entangled with legalism. Their love for others grows cold. Eventually, they lose compassion, and though they know what they ought to do, they have no power to do it.

> We know that the law is spiritual; but I am unspiritual, sold as a slave to sin. I do not understand what I do. For what I want to do I do not do, but what I hate I do.
> —Romans 7:14-15

Before his born-again experience, Paul was a perfect example of one who knew God's commandments but had no power to obey without the Holy Spirit, by faith in Jesus Christ. The letter of the law kills, but God's Spirit gives life.

Legalists can become extremely critical of those who find freedom in Christ. Paul persecuted the Church, threw Christians in prison, and approved death for others—all the while thinking he did the right thing.

This resembles actions of many terrorists. They see American wickedness in our media and feel something must be done! So they "purge" evil, as they are taught. And again, the letter of the law kills, but the Spirit gives life, as 2 Corinthians 3:6 states clearly.

They have no revelation of the Holy Spirit's power to change peoples' lives. God alone, through the power of the Spirit, can change America's wickedness. And it's interesting that terrorists fail to see the terrible hate and evil within themselves. They too need a Savior, as does all mankind.

We, as the Church of Jesus, limit Him by our refusal to stand for righteousness—against evil. Those who refuse the message of faith not only have a problem with sin in their lives, but often also battle depression and diseases as well. We all face these attacks in our lives. But believers who embrace faith have a greater ability to overcome and bear fruit for God's kingdom, despite life's circumstances. Those who reject faith often persecute others who receive it. They join the main accuser of the brethren—Satan—in slander and finding fault. They fail to love and can eventually become suspicious of everyone, expecting people's worst behavior. Many become bitter and resentful. They lose sight of the goodness of God. Indeed, the goodness of God brings about repentance, just as Romans 2:4 says. Jesus said in Luke 6:35 that God is gracious, even to the ungrateful and evil. Still, these religious people do not understand the power of love and forgiveness. This unbelief results in fruitless lives. Churches with these stagnant believers will be full of strife, sickness, and death. Without faith and action, they will have unhealthy fear, which leads to death.

I pray we receive the full counsel of God's Word. And I wish those who are called to different areas of truth might stop criticism of one another. Let's pray they unite in unity and love.

Judgment will eventually come, even to God's house, and the Church of Jesus Christ will be shaken. Only what is built on a solid rock of truth will stand. Then, once God purifies His Church, He will fill her with His presence. When we humble ourselves, God's glory will fill us, and we are His Church. When we weep over our sins with repentance, our mourning will turn into joy, like Psalm 30:5 says. When His Church ceases to be *un*faithful and reaps the final harvest, Jesus will come for His bride.

Are We Hungry Enough for God?

Bread is a symbol of God's presence. The Church is sometimes known as the House of Bread.

> Then Jesus declared, "I am the bread of life. He who comes to me will never go hungry, and he who believes in me will never be thirsty."
> —John 6:35

Bread is also a symbol of Christ's body, sacrificed so we may have eternal life and partake of the bread of life—His divine nature.

> I am the bread of life. Your forefathers ate the manna in the desert, yet they died. But here is the bread that comes down from heaven, which a man may eat and not die. I am the living bread that came down from heaven. If anyone eats of this bread, he will live forever. This bread is my flesh, which I will give for the life of the world.
> —John 6:48-51

The "living bread" is God's presence, the living Word, and the fullness of the Holy Spirit. It includes righteousness, joy, and peace. When we partake, we get His wisdom, holiness, divine health, and prosperity. We receive the very Life of God, and it satisfies our hunger. The question is, are we hungry for this bread?

The choice is ours to partake of the bread of life freely, but are we hungry? Not if our bellies are filled with other food. If we live to satisfy our fleshly appetites, we will be satiated by sensual stimulation.

I know I've tried at times to fill myself with the flesh, and it simply doesn't satisfy. A child of God who attempts to calm his hunger with the world's delights will eventually suffer nausea. So why do people leave churches and return to their life focused totally on the world? They try to satisfy an inner hunger with pleasure alone. Soon they become so intoxicated, they lose a hunger for God. But they also lose peace, joy, and right standing with Him. There is perhaps no one as miserable as a Christian who turns his back on God.

We might ask someone, "Are you really hungry for God?"

"Yes, I am definitely hungry for God," they might reply.

But how hungry are we? Enough to attend church only once a week and never give God another thought? Do cares of the world consume our time, energy, and spoil our appetite for God? Do we have a hobby or interest that crowds our mealtime with the bread of life? At what cost do we hunger for the world? Are we willing to lose peace, joy, and right standing with God? Are we willing to lose our souls?

God looks for those who are not merely hungry, but starving for His bread of life. Let's take a journey in our imaginations to a third-world country and observe people who are desperately hungry. Some of you have actually been there to see them firsthand. Others have seen them on television. See the people who will walk long distances when they hear there is food? See the people—young and old—too weak to walk, who die as a result, while others are fortunate enough to have friends or relatives who bring them food?

Famished people around the world smile with joy and expectation when they hear nourishment is near. And they're willing to wait in long lines for hours. In a panic, some people rush the ones who distribute staples, while stronger individuals compete and fight for portions already given.

When will Christians understand we have heavenly manna that is much better than earthly provisions? Even in America, poor hungry souls look for soul bread. Many attend churches, expecting fulfillment, only to discover emptiness, because some of our churches in

America are dead, void of the manifested presence of God. Hungry people leave empty if a church is unable to satisfy their hunger.

We must fill our churches with the Bread of Life. Away with manmade traditions and men's opinions! Let's return to the Living Word of God. Let's allow God's Spirit free reign in our services. Only then will His House be full of the Bread of Life.

America has been truly blessed with a flood of God's word and revelation. But, have we lost our hunger? Western Europe was once hungry for God. Now, many of these nations no longer believe in a God. There are countries right now starving for the Gospel of Jesus Christ, where people travel for miles to partake of the heavenly bread. In parts of the world, they are willing to risk even death to satisfy their hunger for God.

So, how hungry are we? Are we willing to sacrifice our comfort to obtain the prize of the high calling of God? The Apostle Paul became so hungry for God that he saw everything else as worthless:

> But whatever was to my profit I now consider loss for the sake of Christ. What is more, I consider everything a loss compared to the surpassing greatness of knowing Christ Jesus my Lord, for whose sake I have lost all things. I consider them rubbish, that I may gain Christ…
> —Philippians 3:7-8

Many times we worry and fret about things that really are not important. All temporal things the world strives for will soon pass away. The great missionary Jim Elliot spoke of losing things we cannot keep and seeking what we cannot lose. This is the way of God's kingdom, the way to satisfy a hunger in our souls. So why should we worry and fret? Why should we be in a hurry? Why allow this world to squeeze us into its mold of stress and unrest? Instead, partake of His bread of life.

"Come to me, all you who are weary and burdened, and I will give you rest. Take my yoke upon you and learn from me, for I am gentle and humble in heart, and you will find rest for your souls. For my yoke is easy and my burden is light." Jesus said in Matthew 11:28-30.

His bread of life brings peace and costs us nothing. The blood of the Lamb bought it, to bring rest for our souls. Jesus calls us, His bride. He beckons us to come to Him.

Come Away with Me

While writing this book, I received this message for the Church from the Holy Spirit in February 2004:

Come away with me, my love. Come away from the heavy cares of this world. Come away from the stress. Come away from the striving. You will find me in the simple life with the meek and lowly. I have prepared a feast before you. Come and dine with me. Partake of the bread of life freely. You will find rest for your mind. Let me hold you in my arms. Let me laugh with you and cry with you. Let us dance together. Let me share your most intimate thoughts and I will share with you my thoughts. I love your company. Walk with me in the cool of the day. I will awaken you to the dawn of a new day. Come away with me, my love.

Fruit Inspection

1. List the steps Jesus gives to discipline someone within the Church, from Matthew 18:15-17.

   _____
   _____
   _____
   _____

2. Have you ever been offended with someone in the Church? How did you resolve the conflict?

3. What does Jesus mean when He tells us to treat a fallen person as a publican or heathen?

   Why do you suppose Jesus would say this?

4. Cite examples such as 1 Corinthians 5:9-13 that show how Paul followed the teachings of Christ concerning discipline within the Church.

5. What does Paul mean when he instructs believers in Corinth to purge old leaven?

6. Why is it necessary to do this?

   Can you think of instances when this action was needed in your church?

7. List ways to purge leaven from a church.

8. When we see a fellow believer fall away from Christ, what are the first steps we should take?

9. Does the Holy Spirit ever lead one to confront sin in the life of another?

Why do people refuse to confront sin in their lives and in others?
_____
_____
_____

10. What should our motive be in confronting others?
_____
_____
_____

Does confronting sin help or hurt the people involved?
_____
_____
_____

In what cases can it help? In what cases can it hurt?
_____
_____
_____

11. List steps parents can take to prevent destructive behavior in their children.
_____
_____
_____

Why do parents refuse to take steps of discipline?

12. What does revival within the Church entail?

13. List reasons why much of this generation has not seen true revival.

Why are people in the Church afraid of revival?

14. Which is more important, holiness or prosperity?

Do these contradict one another?

Why or why not?

15. What does it mean to prosper?

    What are factors that bring prosperity?

16. Why is it necessary to receive the message of prosperity as well as holiness?

    What happens if we receive the message of prosperity but reject holiness?

176 • THE GREAT FRUIT INSPECTOR

What happens if we receive holiness but reject faith and prosperity?

_____
_____
_____

17. The 1960s charismatic revival ushered in a new freedom for the Church and great technology advances, like computer automation. How did Satan counteract the positive aspects of this revival?

_____
_____
_____

How can you guard against these devices of the enemy?

_____
_____
_____

18. How hungry are you to know and experience God? When have you set aside time for an appointment with God?

_____
_____
_____

If so, did you keep that appointment?

_____
_____
_____

Chapter 5

JUDGMENT OF RULERS
THE RISE AND FALL OF KINGS

We've discussed how God judges His Church and how we as believers are expected to judge. We have learned how and why God judges individuals by examining their fruit. His motive for judgment is love, to save this world from anarchy, which leads to destruction. Now, let's believe in faith for God's divine revelation concerning rulers of nations.

God is extremely involved in the lives of those who have obtained a place of authority. He takes an interest in how they rule, whether in righteousness or with corruption. God will use them to bring justice and mercy. To accomplish this, He will influence rulers to bring about His plans on the earth. Those with positions of high authority have a greater influence upon society; therefore, they are also held to a higher standard of accountability. Consider these words of wisdom:

> So then, you kings, you rulers the world over, listen to what I say, and learn from it. You govern many lands and are proud that so many people are under your rule, but this authority has been given to you by the Lord Most High. He will examine what

you have done and what you plan to do. You rule on behalf of God and his kingdom, and if you do not govern justly, if you do not uphold the law, if you do not live according to God's will, you will suffer sudden and terrible punishment. Judgment is especially severe on those in power. Common people may be mercifully forgiven for their wrongs, but those in power will face a severe judgment. The Lord of all is not afraid of anyone, no matter how great they are. He himself made everyone, great and common alike, and he provides for all equally, but he will judge the conduct of rulers more strictly.

—Solomon 6:1-8[1]

A Battle for Leaders' Minds

Though God plays a major role in appointing leaders and attempts to influence their decisions, He will not violate free will. They make the final decisions. For example, Pilate had the final word on Jesus' fate. But God knew Pilate's decision, and it fell right into His plans and purposes.

Likewise, Satan attempts to influence rulers to bring about his plans. What is Satan's plan? He simply wants to keep God's Word from coming to pass, to ascend and rule the earth himself. He'd rather see mankind destroyed than see Christ return and reign. Both Satan and the Holy Spirit work to influence our leaders. Yet God always gives men free will, so earth's rulers choose whether to yield to good or to evil.

> Then I saw three evil spirits that looked like frogs; they came out of the mouth of the dragon, out of the mouth of the beast and out of the mouth of the false prophet. They are spirits of demons performing miraculous signs, and they go out to the kings of the whole world, to gather them for the battle on the great day of God Almighty.
>
> —Revelation 16:13-14

These are not miracles to benefit mankind as with God's angels, but miracles of evil and destruction. Even as God's angels work for the good of mankind, angels of darkness work for man's destruction.

> The thief comes only to steal and kill and destroy; I have come that they may have life, and have it to the full.
> —John 10:10

From the tragedy at Waco, Texas, to the bombing in Oklahoma City, to terrorist attacks on the twin towers and the Pentagon, events of evil were brought about by the powers of darkness. In Satan's devious way, these were miracles of deception and precise timing. Upon seeing these terrors unfold, many said, "Unbelievable! Unthinkable!" Without supernatural aid from the destroyer, these atrocious acts might not have been possible. However, the rulers of darkness plant dastardly acts in men's minds and help bring them to pass.

The principalities of darkness deceive and control many leaders on the earth, who yield to them. Without the Spirit of Jesus, a ruler is no match for Satan's strategies. John tells us in Revelation, devils work miracles that set the stage for a final battle in mankind's history. The timing, precision, thoughts, actions, and abilities of those involved are all brought about supernaturally by the powers of darkness.

Various intelligence agencies of the United States disconcertingly shake their heads and wonder how such tragedies can occur. They may be bewildered as to why we were so helpless to stop the attacks. But these same leaders may be oblivious to the fact they were not battling terrorists alone, but devils that influence men, giving them ideas and fanatic abilities.

> For our struggle is not against flesh and blood, but against the rulers, against the authorities, against the powers of this dark world and against the spiritual forces of evil in the heavenly realms.
> —Ephesians 6:12

How can we stop future terrorist activities? Can our great military and intelligence departments prevent them? If we repent as a nation—from the highest leaders down to the smallest child—and turn to God for help, He can give our military supernatural ability like He did for King David's armies.

God is in no great struggle with the devil, as some perhaps believe. Satan is a grain of sand compared to the God of the universe. Men simply allow evil to rule on earth by choosing to live without God and by refusing to obey His Word.

How then does God judge nations and individuals? He does so by lifting His presence away and quietly stepping back. God is a gentleman and will not force Himself on anyone!

"How can God allow such a thing to happen?" people may ask.

"How could *we* allow such a thing to happen?" is what we should say.

If we worship materialism and worldly pleasures, not giving God as much as a thought during the day; if we neglect to study His Word and do what it says; if our heart is turned toward evil, then how can we blame God for our wrongdoing? Yes, God can give our military supernatural ability to fight destruction with destruction, but I submit to you a better way.

Power from Above

As a child and teenager, I remember the Cold War and communist aggression. Long ago I concluded the only way to halt an advance of the Red Army was a massive world war. At that time, I knew very little of spiritual things and the power of God.

In 1983, I experienced a great indwelling of the Holy Spirit, the power Christ spoke of prior to His ascension into heaven, the power to be His witnesses, as in Acts 1:8. For the next five years I joined millions of other saints who prayed earnestly for the Iron Curtain to fall. Then it dawned on me there was a better way to destroy communism than through war. Finally, in 1989, our prayers were answered, and the Iron Curtain fell without a single military offensive!

If terrorists are converted to Christ, it will only be by the hand of the Almighty in response to His people's prayers. Likewise, if our environment is to be saved, it will also be by His hand, in response to His people's prayers. If our education system is to regain its prominence as the best in the world, we must return to the God of our fathers. If we are to stop a relentless wave of crime, we must teach our children the basics of God's truth and His Gospel.

Only through the Gospel of Jesus Christ can men receive power to overcome sin. Our government can spend billions of dollars to stop terrorism, protect our environment, improve education, and stop crime. Yet, if we fail to humble ourselves, seek the Lord, and turn from wickedness, all efforts will be in vain. The spiritual realm always affects our natural realm!

> Some trust in chariots, and some in horses, but we trust in the name of the Lord our God.
> —Psalm 20:7

"Don't you realize I have the power to have you crucified?" Pilate incredulously responded when Jesus refused to answer Pilate's interrogations.

"You would have no power, had it not been given to you from above," Jesus replied in John 19:11, knowing God sets rulers over the nations.

Jesus supported the Scriptures, which make clear God's sovereignty in appointing rulers. Based on God's Word, we can concur He plays a major role in our lives today, whether we know it or not. World leaders can yield to the influence of the Holy Spirit or to evil spirits.

Let's develop this thought further. Throughout history, from Pharaoh and Moses to Hitler and Churchill, we know from the Holy Scriptures God raises leaders and He brings them down. And He also holds them to a higher standard of righteousness, because they influence more people.

> Not many of you should presume to be teachers, my brothers, because you know that we who teach will be judged more strictly.
> —James 3:1

Masters can be translated leaders, rulers, or teachers. This includes leaders of nations, as well as leaders in the Church. God raises rulers and removes them at His pleasure. Their lives and decisions impact nations, so although evil men are not in God's perfect will, He uses them to bring about His purposes. Evil leaders will not intentionally make a tremendous impact in the world for good. Still, God can use their deeds for good. He can and does show forth His power and justice through any manner he wishes.

> The LORD brings death and makes alive; he brings down to the grave and raises up. The LORD sends poverty and wealth; he humbles and he exalts.
> —1 Samuel 2:6-7

It inspires us to hear about righteous leaders like David, Solomon, Joshua and others recorded throughout history. Many books are written about these great men. On the other hand, God has dealt with many evil leaders as well. Let's gain insight on how He deals with unrighteousness.

In Daniel chapter four, we see how God judged a mighty monarch of history. At that time Babylonia was the most powerful empire which ever existed, and Nebuchadnezzar its greatest king. God gave him the wisdom and ability to build an empire. Although he was ruthless and barbaric in battle campaigns, God used his mighty army for His purposes.

This king ruled 45 years. He broke Egypt's power in the famous battle of Carchemish, then crushed a rebellion in Palestine, burning Jerusalem and taking many captives. After he gained dominance over much of the known world, Nebuchadnezzar finally had a chance to reflect on his victories and revel in his affluence.

About this time, the king of Babylon had a dream, which frightened and confused him. Nebuchadnezzar already knew Daniel was a man in whom the Spirit of God dwelled. And Daniel's excellent spirit allowed him to exert great influence over the king, since he had already interpreted previous dreams. So Nebuchadnezzar sent for Daniel, God's beloved prophet, to interpret again.

This dream was about a great tree, which grew high to the heavens. Many birds and animals took refuge in its shade. Then a holy one from heaven came down and proclaimed: "Cut down the tree, cut off his branches, shake off his leaves and scatter his fruit. Let the animals leave the tree, and the birds flee his branches. Nevertheless, leave the stump and let him be covered with dew.

Let his portion be with the beasts and the grass of the earth. Let his heart be changed from a man's to a beast's."

The tree was none other than Nebuchadnezzar, himself. After he obtained unparalleled power over the kingdoms of the world, Nebuchadnezzar became prideful and failed to see it was God who subdued the nations. Then his pride led to other sins, and in his arrogance, he became more cold and cruel. Daniel warned Nebuchadnezzar to change his ways.

> Therefore, O king, be pleased to accept my advice: Renounce your sins by doing what is right, and your wickedness by being kind to the oppressed. It may be that then your prosperity will continue.
>
> —Daniel 4:27

Although God used Nebuchadnezzar to bring judgment upon many nations, he had become full of pride and failed to give any glory to God. Then shunning Daniel's advice, the great king eventually lost his sanity and lived like a wild beast for seven years. This conqueror, once feared and revered, survived in the fields by eating grass. His hair grew long and thick, like eagle feathers, and his nails became like bird's claws. Dew covered his body, exactly as the tree stump in his dream.

As a result, the great King Nebuchadnezzar lost his kingdom. His advisors ruled instead. Finally, after seven years, he repented of his arrogance and gave glory to God. Immediately upon repentance, he regained his senses and the kingdom was restored, but only after he realized who had given him power to conquer nations.

> Now I, Nebuchadnezzar, praise and exalt and glorify the King of heaven, because everything he does is right and all his ways are just. And those who walk in pride he is able to humble.
>
> —Daniel 4:37

Don't Touch My Anointed Ones

Let's consider now the judgment of another king, one who lived during the age of grace under the New Covenant of Jesus Christ. King Herod Aggripa I was son of Herod Antipas who beheaded John the Baptist, and grandson of Herod the Great who murdered the children of Bethlehem in an effort to kill Christ. And like his father and grandfather, this evil son continued to murder God's servants. Acts 12 tells the story of Peter's arrest and deliverance, but James, the brother of John, was not so fortunate. King Herod had James put to death with a sword.

> When he saw that this pleased the Jews, he proceeded to seize Peter also. This happened during the Feast of Unleavened Bread.
> —Acts 12:3

The Jews were pleased with the Apostle James' death. Fearing the opinions of men, King Herod gave in to Jewish pressure, because he wanted to strengthen his power and prestige among Jewish leaders. He later had Peter arrested, but the Church flexed its muscle through the power of prayer, then an angel miraculously set Peter free. Otherwise, he most certainly could have met the same fate as James.

> Fear of man will prove to be a snare, but whoever trusts in the LORD is kept safe.
> —Proverbs 29:25

Herod was a wicked ruler, full of pride and lust for power. Like his father, King Herod did evil for years, yet God gave him plenty of time to repent. As if James' death was not sin enough, Herod added pride to his list. Satan used Herod to hinder the work of early

Christians. But when the Church finally exercised its authority in prayer, Herod received swift judgment.

> And upon a set day Herod, arrayed in royal apparel, sat upon his throne, and made an oration unto them. And the people gave a shout, saying, It is the voice of a god, and not of a man. And immediately the angel of the Lord smote him, because he gave not God the glory: and he was eaten of worms, and gave up the ghost.
> —Acts 12:21-23

This is a clear example of how a nation's leader is held to a higher standard of accountability. God gives time to repent, but if a leader continues in arrogance to oppose God and His saints, he will be brought down. If a leader gets in the way of God's plans, he will be removed! Notice after the death of Herod, God's Word continued to grow. None can stop the Word of God!

A more recent example is how God used Ronald Reagan's leadership to bring down the Soviet empire. In the 1980s, God's people prayed for the Iron Curtain to crumble, but there were seemingly impossible barriers; the largest was the Soviet empire. An amazing sequence of events led the Soviet Union to disband, under the leadership of Gorbachev.

Gorbachev ascended the Communist hierarchy in an atmosphere of growing anxiety among the Soviet leaders, who were concerned about the country's economy and the U.S. military buildup. God prepared Gorbachev from childhood for His purposes. Living on his father's farm, he faced a tough childhood during the brutal reign of Stalin. However, Gorbachev excelled on the farm and in the classroom. His intelligence and leadership caught the attention of the Soviet elite. He was able to attend Moscow University and study law before entering the Communist Party of the Soviet

Union. His career moved forward rapidly as he worked his way up to the CPSU Central Committee.

In the meantime, Brezhnev agreed to hold historic talks on nuclear disarmament with President Nixon and the U.S. However, Nixon's abrupt resignation dealt the peace talks a severe blow. It is likely that the Soviets perceived this as American weakness. As a result, the Cold War continued with increased Soviet aggression. Gorbachev was promoted to the Politburo and received full membership in 1980, the same year Ronald Reagan was elected President of the United States. God was arranging His leaders for His divine purposes. Reagan proved to be a strong leader and worked to end the world's perception of a weak America.

Yuri Andropov briefly succeeded Brezhnev, who died in November 1982. Andropov promoted Gorbachev to second in command. Although Gorbachev had obtained much favor with Andropov, the Soviet leader was unable to move Chernenko out of the line of succession before his health gave out in February 1984. Chernenko replaced Andropov as Soviet leader, but he too died little more than one year after taking office. Following Cherneko's death, Gorbachev quickly won the endorsement of the Politburo and was elected General Secretary of the Communist Party. The world stage was set with the proper actors for God's purposes. Through these leaders' efforts, a significant turn in history was about to unfold.

Gorbachev initiated programs of reform including perestroika and glasnost, designed to bring greater freedoms to the Soviet Union. His attempts of reform, as well as his summit conferences with President Reagan, contributed to the end of the Cold War and also ended the political power of the Communist Party of the Soviet Union, leading to the its collapse.

In fewer than three years, the Soviet Union had four different leaders until God brought the right one into position for His plans- Mikhail Gorbachev. Brezhnev, Andropov, and Chernenko all died of diseases. But was it merely a series of unfortunate coincidences?

Or could it be an angel of the Lord who struck these leaders, as he did Herod?

It was not God's perfect will for these men to perish, but perhaps it resulted from natural and spiritual laws. Could it be that God allowed spiritual and natural laws to take effect in their lives, without intervening? Since these men didn't know Him or even believe in a God, the One whom they determined did not exist did not save them from their fate. God refused to override their free will.

The law of sin and death operated in their lives. And like Herod, these Soviet leaders prevented the Gospel from being proclaimed, and their KGB persecuted saints. Did God bring judgment to protect those in the Soviet Union with whom He was in a covenant?

Whatever His reasoning, one thing is certain—God worked the death of these Soviet leaders for His purposes and for His glory! Soon the ripe fields of souls in the Soviet Empire began to ripen for harvest.

In addition, the Soviet economy dropped into bankruptcy, while competing in the arms race with America, led by President Reagan. Although Reagan drew criticism from most of Europe and many Americans, he courageously stood his ground on foreign policy.

> Fear of man will prove to be a snare, but whoever trusts in the LORD is kept safe.
> —Proverbs 29:25

As in the book of Acts, the Word of the Lord continued to grow in the Soviet Empire. It will happen again in the last days, when the anti-Christ and the leaders of the nations set themselves against believers and against the nation of Israel. The anti-Christ will be allowed to prevail for a time as part of God's judgment of the nations, but not for long.

They will make war against the Lamb, but the Lamb will overcome them because he is Lord of lords and King of kings—and with him will be his called, chosen and faithful followers. For God has put it into their hearts to accomplish his purpose by agreeing to give the beast their power to rule, until God's words are fulfilled.
—Revelation 17:14, 17

Evil Rulers

The question may arise, "Why does God allow evil rulers to come into power? After all, doesn't God appoint all rulers and governments?"

Everyone must submit himself to the governing authorities, for there is no authority except that which God has established. The authorities that exist have been established by God.
—Romans 13:1

Authority in this verse refers to a king or individuals who make the laws of the land and enforce them. God does appoint authorities to bring peace and stability. But what about those authorities who bring evil, unrest, and oppression? Does God appoint evil men? To answer this let's see what Jesus said in Matthew 19, when Pharisees asked Him if it was lawful for a man to put away his wife:

"Haven't you read," he replied, "that at the beginning the Creator 'made them male and female,' and said, 'For this reason a man will leave his father and mother and be united to his wife, and the two will become one flesh'? So they are no longer two, but one. Therefore what God has joined together, let man not separate." "Why then," they asked, "did Moses command that a man give his wife a certificate of divorce and send her away?" Jesus replied,

> "Moses permitted you to divorce your wives because your hearts were hard. But it was not this way from the beginning."
> —Matthew 19:4-8

For the same reason God allowed men to put away their wives during the time of Moses, He allows wicked rulers. He gives man free will; then men choose what and whom to follow. Rebellion and hard hearts allow evil governments into power.

A good example of this is found in 1 Samuel 8. Walking in God's counsel, Samuel ruled Israel wisely, but his sons ruled dishonestly, taking bribes, loving money. Israel's elders didn't want Samuel's sons to rule over them, so they demanded Samuel give them a king. Look at God's reply:

> And the LORD told him: "Listen to all that the people are saying to you; it is not you they have rejected, but they have rejected me as their king."
> —1 Samuel 8:7

Notice, when a person rejects the advice and warnings of God's prophet, he doesn't reject the prophet; he rejects God, Himself. God could have raised another man to rule Israel, instead of Samuel's sons. But Israel's people failed to trust Him. So God allowed them to have what they wanted, because He knew their hearts were set on a king, whether or not He approved.

God warned of troubles inherited with a king, like heavy taxes and their children becoming servants, two hardships mentioned in the Bible. Nevertheless, He appointed them a king, as they desired. Later, God worked around their unwise choices to bring about His plans, through David and Solomon, ushering in the greatest period of prosperity in Israel's history. What a marvelous answer to poor choices.

God loves us as much today and will work around our foolish choices to bring about His plans. He works on behalf of those who love Him to give them the greatest possible blessings our choices will allow, as in Romans 8:28. This is God's love.

We are to submit to those whom God has appointed over us. This includes authorities in church, government, jobs, at home, at school, and sports team coaches. We are to treat all these people over us with utmost respect, so *we* won't fall into judgment.

> Everyone must submit himself to the governing authorities, for there is no authority except that which God has established. The authorities that exist have been established by God. Consequently, he who rebels against the authority is rebelling against what God has instituted, and those who do so will bring judgment on themselves.
> —Romans 13:1-2

Paul speaks of rebellion here. If we resist our authorities, we risk judgment on ourselves! On the other hand, we are not to compromise God's commandments either. If a conflict arises between governing authorities and God's Word, there is little doubt what we should choose.

Most of us know of the story of the three Hebrews who refused to bow to King Nebuchadnezzar's golden image. They didn't rebel against the king or his authority. They simply refused to disobey God's commandments, and they made no apologies.

> Shadrach, Meshach and Abednego replied to the king, "O Nebuchadnezzar, we do not need to defend ourselves before you in this matter. If we are thrown into the blazing furnace, the God we serve is able to save us from it, and he will rescue us from your hand, O king. But even if he does not, we want you to know, O

king that we will not serve your gods or worship the image of gold you have set up."

—Daniel 3:16-18

Sometimes God may require us to stand against godless laws, policies, or leaders. There may come a time in our country's decline when we must take a stand for what we believe, even if it means fines, imprisonment, or death. But what's more important, our comfort or God's plan? The three young Hebrews chose God. What if a work manager asks us to compromise what the Word of God makes clear? Again, what's more important, our security or God's righteousness? If godless leaders pass godless laws, who are we to obey? If those in authority order us to do something we know is wrong, what do we do? The apostles faced this dilemma when the rulers of Jerusalem imprisoned them.

A lame man, crippled since birth, was miraculously healed at the temple through the ministry of Peter and John. No doubt this caused a big stir among the people! Peter boldly stood in the temple preaching the gospel, and about five thousand were saved. The rulers and chief priests heard about this great miracle and had the apostles arrested. When these same rulers saw the man who had been miraculously healed, they could not deny it, but they commanded the apostles to cease speaking about Jesus. So they were faced with a decision to obey and stop preaching truth or not to obey.

> But Peter and John replied, "Judge for yourselves whether it is right in God's sight to obey you rather than God. For we cannot help speaking about what we have seen and heard."
>
> —Acts 4:19-20

Did the apostles rebel against authority? No, their authorities rebelled against God. The apostles made the right choice. What if godless leaders in our nation make godless laws and render unjust decisions in our courts? We each need to determine, is it right in the sight of God, to obey them or not?

A Few Good Men

God examines a person and searches his heart, before promoting or demoting him. But what does God look for in a leader? What are His criteria?

He is courageous, which means:

- He is not afraid to make a decision. (Joshua 1:6-11)
- He's not constantly worried or fretful. (Psalm 37:8, Philippians 4:6-7)
- He's not frozen by anxiety. (James 1:5-8)
- He does not act in haste. (Proverbs 14:29, Proverbs 21:5)
- He does not procrastinate. (Proverbs 24:10)
- He patiently seeks God's wisdom. (Proverbs 24:5-6, Proverbs 15:22)
- He is willing to step out, in faith. (Hebrews 10:38)
- He's not afraid to take a few risks. (Matthew 25:14-30)
- He is quiet and confident. (Isaiah 32:17)
- He searches for the truth of a matter, before a final decision. (Proverbs 25:2)
- He's aggressive, when needed. (Proverbs 12:24, Matthew 11:12)
- He receives wisdom from God and takes decisive action, when appropriate. (1 Kings 3:16-28)
- He stands with his decision, in faith, without wavering. (Numbers 14:6-9, Hebrews 10:35-36)
- He hates wickedness and loves honesty. (Proverbs 16:12-13)

Second, a good leader is humble, which means:

- He admits his mistakes. (Proverbs 25:12)
- He corrects his errors. (Proverbs 13:18)
- He knows God is the only perfect one. (Deuteronomy 32:4)
- He studies God's Word, for wisdom. (Joshua 1:7-8)
- He acts with honesty and integrity. (Proverbs 16:13)
- He rules justly. (Proverbs 16:10, Proverbs 24:24-25)
- He doesn't take his position lightly. (James 3:1)
- He has a healthy fear of God. (Proverbs 1:7)
- He is teachable. (Proverbs 9:8-9)
- He is willing to accept correction. (Proverbs 12:1, Proverbs 15:31-33)
- He respects and esteems the wise. (Proverbs 14:35)
- He walks with the wise. (Proverbs 13:20)
- He doesn't take counsel from the ungodly, but from God's Word. (Psalm 1:1-2)

Finally, a good leader must act unselfishly, willing to serve others. Unlike the world, the greatest in the kingdom of God is one who serves the most.

God is the Supreme Servant, as demonstrated by the Messiah, when He came to earth as a servant of both God and man. God is the Great Servant. Jesus' example is the one we are to follow. He turned water into wine at the wedding of Cana. He washed his disciples' feet. He died on the cross. These acts all demonstrated His attitude of service.

We, as Christians, are to behave with this same attitude. A leader appointed by God must live unselfishly, willing to sacrifice. He's not troubled by inconvenience, interruptions, or problems to solve.

What about leaders who make major mistakes? What about those with character flaws? How about those who are evil? Why are they allowed to rise to power? If they possess good leadership qualities, those may be reasons God allows them to rule. Also, God sometimes uses evil leaders to bring judgment upon nations, as in the case of Nebuchadnezzar.

God will search nations to find qualified leaders. He will appoint men to suit His purpose. But God limits His own interference in the affairs of men, watching the faith and prayers of His saints. Remember, God is love and will not force His will on anyone.

While God has appointed leaders, they are not to make themselves gods over the lives of others. Authorities in government and the Church are to walk humbly before both God and men. Greater authority means a greater opportunity to *serve*. They must always remain open for correction, no matter what position they have. God can use the innocent question of a small child to correct a great leader. He can also use a donkey to correct a prophet, as in the story of Balaam, in Numbers 22. But we are always to think with caution when judging others, especially leaders.

> Watch out for false prophets. They come to you in sheep's clothing, but inwardly they are ferocious wolves. By their fruit you will recognize them. Do people pick grapes from thorn bushes, or figs from thistles? Likewise every good tree bears good fruit, but a bad tree bears bad fruit. A good tree cannot bear bad fruit, and a bad tree cannot bear good fruit. Every tree that does not bear good fruit is cut down and thrown into the fire. Thus, by their fruit you will recognize them.
> —Matthew 7:15-20

God discerns not by appearance, but by the heart. We don't even know what is in our own hearts unless God reveals it to us. This is why the psalmist asks God,

> Search me, O God, and know my heart; test me and know my anxious thoughts. See if there is any offensive way in me, and lead me in the way everlasting.
> —Psalm 139:23-24

If we don't even know what's in our own hearts, how can we know what's in the hearts of others, unless God reveals it to us as we observe their fruit? God raises leaders and destroys them, at will. Much of it depends on the prayers of His saints, as we read in 1 Timothy 2:1-2; Ezekiel 22:30; Matthew 18:19. Always remember, God gives every person free will. If the Church will pray and ask, God will listen in the affairs of nations.

Fruit Inspection

1. What role does God have in appointing leaders? (Psalm 75: 6-7)

   _____
   _____
   _____

   (John 19:10-11)

   _____
   _____
   _____

2. Why does God judge leaders and ministers more strictly than others? (James 3:1)

   _____
   _____
   _____

3. How does God influence leaders?

   _____
   _____

JUDGMENT OF RULERS • 197

What are Satan's devices to influence leaders?

4. How do you think communist aggression was stopped?

   How do you suppose terrorism will be defeated?

5. Why did King Nebuchadnezzar lose his authority as king of Babylon?

   Why was it restored to him? (Daniel 4)

Why did God judge King Herod Aggripa I? (Acts 12:21-23)

6. From these examples, what is the main reason for a ruler's downfall?

Why will nations' leaders align themselves with the antichrist, to fight Jesus when He returns to earth?

7. Does God appoint evil rulers?

If God does not appoint evil rulers, how do they get to power?

8. Are we, as Christians, always to submit to those in authority over us?

   Why or Why not? (Romans 13:1-2)

   (Hebrews 13:17)

   (1 Peter 2:13-14)

   (Daniel 3:16-18)

   (Acts 4:19-20)

Discuss specific examples:

9. Are we to refuse submission to anyone who is ill-tempered or doesn't like us? (I Peter 2:18)

10. What are characteristics God looks for in a leader?

How can you become a better leader?

11. How does leadership relate to a family? (Colossians 3:18-21)

Give examples of good leadership within a home, based on these characteristics.

12. Are wives always to submit to their husbands?

Why or why not?

Give examples of appropriate and inappropriate submission.

CHAPTER 6

JUDGMENTS FOR NATIONS
SPEAK TO THE NATIONS

We've discussed judgment of individuals, judgment of the Church body, and judgment of rulers. A fourth realm of God's judgment involves nations. Judgment begins once a nation turns its back on God. Then it gradually or, in some instances, swiftly slips into gross darkness. Without God's power we tend to drift into evil. We open ourselves to principalities of darkness. When people forsake the Lord as a nation, this allows rulers of darkness to have greater influence. In this condition, men who yield to this darkness will rise in power. The Bible refers to dark powers that control evil leaders and nations as "princes of darkness."

DANIEL VERSUS THE PRINCE OF PERSIA

An example of a prince of darkness is seen in the book of Daniel. The prophet Daniel had been praying and fasting for three weeks. He mourned Judah's captivity. Daniel, a man of wisdom, had spent a lifetime studying Scripture. He was aware from Jeremiah's prophecies, where God promised to return Judah after seventy years of captivity, as chapter 29 shows.

It seemed impossible for this prophecy to come to pass, so Daniel pleaded with God on behalf of his people. He interceded with prayer and supplication. Daniel confessed the sins of Judah, asking for mercy and pardon. As a result of those prayers, an angel of God appeared to him in a vision:

> Then he continued, "Do not be afraid, Daniel. Since the first day that you set your mind to gain understanding and to humble yourself before your God, your words were heard, and I have come in response to them. But the prince of the Persian kingdom resisted me twenty-one days. Then Michael, one of the chief princes, came to help me, because I was detained there with the king of Persia."
> —Daniel 10:12-13

The angel made reference to the "prince" of Persia. How was this power of darkness subdued? The evil of Persia experienced defeat by one of God's mighty angels. This demonstrates the importance of prayer in determining the destiny of nations. Through his prayers, Daniel was instrumental in the restoration of Jerusalem. His prayers led to breaking the principalities of darkness over Persia. Perhaps others also prayed, but the prayer of Daniel is recorded for us.

Once the darkness over Persia broke, God appointed Cyrus as king. God then moved upon Cyrus, and as king he sent a proclamation, which allowed the Jews to rebuild the temple of God, as Ezra and Nehemiah tell. So with the help of Daniel's prayers, the prophecies of Jeremiah were fulfilled.

God waited for a man to intercede for the Jews so He could reestablish His temple and bring His people back to Jerusalem. Likewise, God waits for His people of this generation to intercede and decree so He can establish His kingdom on earth.

One way God establishes His kingdom is by exposing works of darkness. Many people are deceived to believe Satan's lies today.

During the Great Tribulation in the future the beast, false prophet, and antichrist will deceive most people. But the Spirit of Christ is the spirit of prophecy, which will bring into light all that is done in darkness and will show us the error of our ways.

Who's in Control?

Different types of principalities control nations, of which many are in spiritual captivity. These principalities blind people to truth, which will set them free. The Holy Spirit wants to expose these powers of darkness and break the bondage. A few powers have the most influence on our present day society.

First is the spirit of control: Communism, totalitarianism, dictatorships, and humanism fall under this principality. Usually intellectual in nature, this spirit is motivated by pride. Governments that operate on this premise think a few bureaucrats are wiser than the rest of the nation. Therefore, since the rest of the nation has no opportunity to make choices, the government does so and enforces what it deems best for an entire society. In essence, they declare themselves gods. Most atheists are good examples, believing themselves the final authority.

This spirit of control will do almost anything to maintain power, sometimes marked by cruelty, with little compassion for human rights. A regimented ruler is unyielding, allows no freedom, and resists all who disagree. Everyone is a pawn of the state or the dictator and must sacrifice for the state's welfare. Those influenced by this spirit see people not as valuable human beings, created in the image of God, but as expendable products. They repress religious freedom and force people to worship the dictator or the nation. Examples include Nazi Germany and the imperial nation of Japan before World War II. More recent examples of this type of principality are the Soviet Union, North Korea, China, and Iraq, under Saddam Hussein's leadership. The spirit of control influences

United State's judges, politicians, and other leaders too. To overcome this spirit, we must be bold, break the bonds of intimidation, and be clothed with humility.

A second type of principality controlling nations is "religion." This principality has characteristics similar to the spirit of control. For instance, instead of worshipping the state, these people worship a religion void of the one true God, without a personal relationship with God through Jesus Christ. And like the spirit of control, a "religious" spirit is repressive, allowing little freedom and no liberty. Instead, people are forced to obey men's laws and traditions, which demonstrates they do not know the one true God of mercy and compassion.

Because God is love, He will not force His will on anyone, and that includes those deceived by a repressive spirit of darkness. God loves those deceived by this evil ruler of darkness. While it's true God will judge people and nations, He will also forgive and pardon if we cry out to Him.

However, those ruled by the spirit of "religion" fail to see forgiveness is in Christ. This prince of darkness is cruel, void of compassion, exactly like a spirit of control, and is motivated by pride and hate. Their "religious" laws aren't written on the heart, so their religion is legalistic, impractical, and impossible to obey.

Like the Pharisees, leaders of this type of government are spiritually blind guides trying to lead a nation of spiritually blind men, as Jesus said in Matthew 15:14. Pride makes them think they are better than others; therefore, they fail to realize a need for the Savior as well. They scrutinize faults and shortcomings of others, but fail to see their own sins. Consequently, they feel justified in oppressing others.

Taken to an extreme, these kinds of leaders think they are justified to murder for their "faith," never realizing they are simply a pawn of evil princes of "religion." Only God's love and saints' prayers can topple these rulers of darkness.

A third type of evil spirit that rules nations is a spirit of poverty found in many third world countries. The driving force of this spirit is hopelessness. Those under its influence always expect the worst and cannot see beyond their present circumstances. They are without hope and see no way out.

Nations in this circumstance accept their wretched condition of poverty as normal. Most serve primitive gods with ancient traditions and religions. Even their so-called Christian churches are often void of a personal relationship with Christ. The spirit of poverty beats people down. Then, having grown weary, they have little strength to help themselves and lack drive or ambition. They've grown passive without revelation of God's willingness to change their circumstances. They learn to depend on governments or other nations like America to feed and help them.

The dark spirit of poverty blinds people to ideas and inventions. Many in such nations are intelligent people, but they perish for lack of knowledge. People under poverty often have no knowledge of God's Word at all, so they break His commandments daily without even realizing it. They don't know right from wrong, in God's sight. Lawlessness abounds. They bring themselves under a curse, ignorant of the Christ who redeemed and set them free.

The atmosphere in these nations is permeated with unbelief. Their governments are usually corrupt, accepting bribes, ruling with little character. They lack courage, wisdom, and other qualities of great leaders. These governments are often dependent, yielding control to nations who give the most aid. This darkness of poverty is only overcome by great faith in a greater God!

The final ruler of darkness we'll examine is the capitalist spirit, which is characterized by pride, greed and discontentment. This spirit rules in most democracies and wealthy nations of the earth. Their people serve the gods of materialism, comfort, and entertainment. And totally unlike nations in poverty, these have tremendous drive and force. With so much ambition, they become powder kegs of stress, ready to explode at any moment. These nations have the highest crime rates and profess themselves free, yet they are bound and imprisoned by appetites for pleasure.

These people practice narcissism, engrossed in love for themselves. They stop at nothing, even to satisfy unnatural desires, whether it hurts or destroys others. Honor, courage, and sacrifice are forgotten relics. They look at honesty, purity, commitment, and decency as outdated bondage.

Many nations in the world were previously Christian, but they have forsaken God to worship pleasures. Like the spirit of control, this principality of darkness entails humanism. They pride themselves in education and technology, with no need for a Supreme Being.

"Mankind does not need God's help. Men are gods, rulers of the universe!" they say.

It's true those in Christ will one day rule the nations, though we can do nothing apart from Him. But the prideful don't know it, nor will they submit to His lordship.

These nations are marked by gross darkness and lawlessness. And out of this darkness, the Antichrist will arise, a principality referred to in Scripture as Babylon, the great harlot, in Revelation 17:3-5. Having known of God and the Gospel of Christ, these nations now forsake Him to worship materialism and entertainment.

People grow fearful and weak because they dread losing the world's pleasures, so they compromise truth; they stand for nothing. These nations are cowardly, without fortitude. They shrink from confrontation and appease evil to maintain comfort. They are blind and don't see that appeasement eventually leads to destruction. They don't understand sacrifice or endurance. Fear perverts their wisdom, and they deny the power of any form of godliness. Professing themselves wise, they have become fools, says Romans 1:22-32. Though claiming to know God, they practice all sorts of perversion.

True believers are labeled extremists, right-wing fanatics, and Bible thumpers. During the tribulation, Christians will be persecuted the most by civilized, high-tech countries, who will attempt to appease the Antichrist. Controlled by a spirit of greed, these nations will face judgment and destruction, enduring the worst of the seven-year tribulation period. Only those who practice self-denial, self-control, and simple devotion to God can overcome the powerful darkness of greed.

All these different principalities and rulers of darkness have power to control nations today. As the tribulation period draws near, their control will increase. But people or nations who follow them will eventually face God's judgment. Since God gives all people freedom to choose how they live and whom they worship and serve, we are each held accountable for allowing darkness any power in our lives.

How God Judges

God has a pattern of bringing judgment to nations, and His ways are perfect. Hebrews 13:8 tells us God is the same yesterday, today and forever; He never changes.

> See, today I appoint you over nations and kingdoms to uproot and tear down, to destroy and overthrow, to build and to plant.
> —Jeremiah 1:10

God usually sent His men and women to warn of coming judgments. Yet some nations became so wicked, no prophets were sent to warn them of impending doom. I'm sure God dealt with at least a few people in warning, but they too refused to listen. Even prophets were sometimes too wicked to hear and obey, as in Ezekiel 22:30. So if no one else stood in the gap, no one to surrender to God as His spokesperson and intercessor, judgment was rendered.

In ancient Israel, God continually sent His spokesmen to warn—men and women referred to as prophets, preachers, or evangelists. Throughout history, spokesmen for the Almighty were persecuted for preaching truth and righteousness. But most refused to back down or give up; they feared God rather than men.

The world today has other names for these messengers: doomsday preachers, Bible thumpers, religious fanatics, religious right-wingers, and radical extremists. These derisive names are given to God's people by prideful, lukewarm, and rebellious ones, unwilling to repent and give God glory.

For years, God will warn of judgments because He is patient and long suffering, not willing for any to perish, but for all to be delivered into eternal life. If a nation still refuses to repent and seek the Lord, He may send minor judgments as further warning, like natural disasters of earthquakes, famine, severe weather, and fires. Judgment may also come in disease, fighting, violence, or invasion by a foreign army.

We need to remember, the spiritual realm affects our natural realm. So judgments must come to pass when spiritual laws are violated and corrupt seeds are sown.

Does God desire or enjoy all of these disasters? By no means, says Ezekiel 18:32! However, He ordained spiritual laws before the foundations of the earth. So there is no way to stop these laws from taking effect except through repentance and deliverance, by the power of Jesus Christ. God may send minor judgments in hopes a nation will awaken from its wandering and humbly come to Him in repentance. All the while, God continues to warn through His prophets.

If any nation stubbornly, continually refuses to repent, God has no alternative but to allow catastrophic judgments. God is love. But love will not sit idle while mankind heads for destruction and hell. God will act to save His righteous, those with whom He is in covenant.

God is also holy; He cannot fellowship with darkness. If a nation chooses perversion, His presence will depart from that nation, allowing the destroyer to wreak destruction. God waits for His saint's prayers so He may show Himself strong upon the earth. He will take action to preserve righteousness. He will do everything possible to reach those whose hearts are hard.

All the while, Satan deceives; he tries to get men to reject God and His commandments. But God is holy and will withdraw His presence if evil continues unabated. Still Satan waits; he looks for any opening to sneak into a life and destroy.

Once the cup of God's anger is full, His wrath will pour upon nations who reject His justice, truth, and mercy. Even still, during the most severe judgments, God will always save and preserve a remnant of His righteous people.

Once the process of judgment is complete among any people, God shows compassion and restores them. When they are humbled and repent, He takes immediate steps of reconciliation.

We see this pattern of God's discipline many times in Scripture, like in Noah's generation. In the book of Judges, we see the pattern repeated again and again with Israel: People forgot God and His Word. They worshipped idols and committed every sort of evil. Yet God still sent prophets and gave plenty of time to repent.

Finally, He allowed enemies to overtake them. Once enslaved, Israel always cried out to God for mercy—eventually. He always heard, then intervened on their behalf. He raised judges like Samson and Gideon to deliver His people; then they lived in peace.

Eventually they forgot and became rebellious, so God allowed enslavement, and the cycle began again. Israel repeated this pattern many times: rebellion, invasion, slavery, repentance, deliverance, restoration, and peace.

Deception Brings Judgment

Another good example of this pattern is in the Bible in Jeremiah and Lamentations. God used Israel's enemies to bring judgment. As we saw in the story of Nebuchadnezzar in 2 Kings, Chapters 24 and 25, God raised a Babylonian army to bring judgment upon many nations, including Judah. This army conquered swift and fierce, showing little mercy.

God's prophet Jeremiah repeatedly warned Judah of judgment. He denounced their idolatry, hypocrisy, and injustice. Yet they refused to repent.

"You are always prophesying negative things," they argued with Jeremiah. "No harm will come to us. Are we not God's chosen people? God will cause us to prosper."

They totally ignored the fact of continual rebellion against God's commandments. Jeremiah was not moved, but continued to warn of approaching discipline. Yet even in the midst of dire warnings, God graciously promised He would one day restore Judah.

After bringing judgment, God always restores and reconciles. Most of Jeremiah's prophecies were filled with judgment and doom. Nevertheless, God countered their dire circumstances with many expressions of tenderness and steadfast love, which we read throughout Jeremiah's book. Still, he was mocked, ridiculed, misunderstood.

When Judah's king read Jeremiah's prophecies, he threw them into a fire. So God told Jeremiah to rewrite the entire book, all the prophecies. Any writer can appreciate Jeremiah's determination, tenacity, and possible frustration.

Israel's officers accused Jeremiah of treason, claiming he sided with the Babylonian army, and they eventually threw him into prison. Blinded by pride, they were truly convinced Jeremiah was not a prophet of God, since they only believed in God's prosperity, not in His discipline or correction. But God patiently waited for His people. He repeatedly warned them to repent, even though they persecuted His prophets.

Finally, a day came when God's cup of wrath against Judah was full. He had to judge them, to spare the few righteous who remained. Had God not allowed judgment, His righteousness might have vanished from the earth.

Jeremiah's warning finally came to pass. The Babylonian army overran Jerusalem, God's city. Then sadly, Judah became a nation of desolation.

> I am the man who has seen affliction by the rod of his wrath. He has driven me away and made me walk in darkness rather than light; indeed, he has turned his hand against me again and again, all day long. He has made my skin and my flesh grow old and has broken my bones. He has besieged me and surrounded me with bitterness and hardship. He has made me dwell in darkness like those long dead. He has walled me in so I cannot escape; he has weighed me down with chains.
> —Lamentations 3:1-7

JESUS PROPHESIES JUDGMENT

Some theologians and Bible teachers imply God will not judge His people with affliction. They reason God is good and will never punish even those who reject Him. This line of reasoning also rejects any belief in hell or a lake of fire.

It's true Jesus went about doing only good while here on earth, as Acts 10:38 tells us. We never find Jesus cursing anyone or sending a catastrophe upon a person. He rebuked James and John when they wanted to send fire down on Samaria. It wasn't the Spirit of God, but an evil spirit of prideful revenge that motivated James and John to call for destruction on Samaria, shown in Luke 9:54-56.

Nevertheless, Jesus did prophesy destruction on several cities of His generation, including Jerusalem, as in Matthew 11:20-24. How could Christ, if He came into the world to do only good, prophecy destruction over cities?

The fact is Jesus knew the inhabitants of these cities would reject Him as Messiah. He knew they would choose death over life. Notice these judgments didn't come until after He left earth. So as long as His Light was with them, the people in these cities were spared. As soon as He departed and returned to heaven from where He came, destruction followed.

From this example, we see how God's presence keeps us from evil and destruction. He is holy and cannot fellowship with evil, and judgment comes when He withdraws His presence, leaving no divine protection. When necessary, God does allow spiritual laws to take effect, without intervening.

If we continually sow corrupt seeds as a nation, we will reap destruction, unless we repent and call upon the God of our fathers. Remember, God will not force Himself on anyone. If we choose to reject Him, He will allow us to do so, to our own demise. But in mercy, He gives us plenty of time to repent and choose life. Consider these words of Jeremiah:

> He has filled me with bitter herbs and sated me with gall. He has broken my teeth with gravel; he has trampled me in the dust. I have been deprived of peace; I have forgotten what prosperity is. So I say, "My splendor is gone and all that I had hoped from the LORD." I remember my affliction and my wandering, the bitterness and the gall. I well remember them, and my soul is downcast within me.
> —Lamentations 3:15-20

God has allowed affliction in the past and will in the future, as Revelation 13:9-10 tells us. He may even lead His people into what seem to be difficult circumstances, as Acts 9:16 shows. Still, there are many unwilling to accept this truth. Even clergy sometimes have trouble with it.

Many ministers have received marvelous revelation concerning healing, God's love, and other truths. Nevertheless, they are blinded concerning afflictions. Perhaps it's because they have never seriously rebelled against God. Maybe they've never known the consuming fire of an angry God. Perhaps His Spirit has never led them into the wilderness.

"We look not at the things seen, but things unseen," says 2 Corinthians 4:18. We need to learn to see through spiritual eyes at eternity, rather than in our limited realm of the flesh. Believers often haven't considered everything our great Shepherd taught. But it will be less painful to go to heaven without a hand, than to end up in hell with both. Similarly, we'd have more joy in heaven with only one eye, than to be tormented forever with two.

The Bible teaches these essential truths:

- It's better to endure affliction, hardship, and discipline than to die in sin. (Hebrews 12:5-9)
- Destruction of the flesh is less painful than destruction of the soul. (Matthew 10:28)
- God's judgment now is better than in the life hereafter. (1 Corinthians 11:31-32)

Rebellion is the rejection of Jesus as Lord and Messiah. Another form of rebellion is when a child of God knows clearly what to do or not to do, but makes a deliberate choice to disobey. I have known the darkness of disobedience. God's best is that we obey Him and prosper. However, prospering does not mean He will never lead us into affliction. God desires we walk with Him and learn to hear His voice. He desires that we prosper and live in peace.

> For he does not willingly bring affliction or grief to the children of men.
> —Lamentations 3:33

If we continue to rebel against God and reject truth, we will face judgment. The wonderful news is we can repent and be cleansed by Jesus Christ's blood! Once we truly repent and return to our Father, he waits to receive us; He waits to forgive; He waits to bless and comfort.

In the book of Lamentations, Jeremiah mourns over Jerusalem's destruction. Then God comforted the righteous who remained. These promises are true:

- God's anger lasts only for a moment, but His mercy endures forever. (Psalm 30:5)
- He will always reach out to comfort those who mourn. (Matthew 5:4)
- He makes His home with those who are humble in heart. (Psalm 34:18)
- He is always there for those who'll admit they need Him. (Psalm 86:5-7)
- When we turn from wickedness to Him, God will comfort and restore. (Isaiah 57:17-19)

Yet this I call to mind and therefore I have hope: Because of the LORD'S great love we are not consumed, for his compassions never fail. They are new every morning; great is your faithfulness. I say to myself, "The LORD is my portion; therefore I will wait for him."

—Lamentations 3:21-24

God Will Correct America

We see this pattern of discipline in the United States. In the mid-to-late 1700s our colonies went through a great revival. From this a tide of freedom surged, and people won independence from Britain's aristocracy. Americans could govern and worship as they pleased and placed great emphasis on sovereign states and individual freedom, based on the Bible. From this foundation, our Constitution was penned, also based on biblical spiritual principles.

Soon after their newfound freedom and prosperity, Americans allowed practices displeasing to God. The spirit of greed exerted its influence in the early 1800s, and many Americans coveted Native American land. Their thoughts were much like the Pharisees': *We are better than the heathen Americans Indians. Are we not entitled to Indian land? After all, we are Christian people. Aren't the American Natives inferior?* Granted, some Native Americans also did horrible acts to the colonists. But instead of forgiving and trying to evangelize them with the gospel, many Americans attempted to annihilate them.

This line of thinking was also prevalent in Nazi Germany, which justified the ensuing horrific holocaust. Similarly, American colonists felt justified to force Indians to leave their homes and move west. Some people treated Indians as lower in value than animals, acting like there wasn't enough room for both. Deceived Americans had an "out of my way" mentality and acted on it. They bowed to the god of materialism. Their greed forced Native Americans to walk the "Trail of Tears" to the West, uprooted, with many dying in the process.

Later, greed flourished in slavery to support industry. Though many men fought for freedom from England, they felt justified to take African peoples' freedom. Then masters mistreated their servants, for profit. So God raised men like Charles Finney, the great revivalist. Under his preaching, many people were convicted of their sin and repented. Harriet Stowe was inspired to write *Uncle Tom's Cabin*, which stirred more people to repent. She and Charles Finney, among others, cried out against the indecency of slavery.

Other preachers cried out against the harsh treatment of American Indians, as a revival fire was kindled. However, it grew too late to stop corrupt seeds sown in the past, and greed plunged our nation into civil war. Tremendous suffering occurred on both sides, especially in the South.

After the process of judgment was complete, God brought a brief period of comfort to our nation. Men like Dwight Moody led great revivals of that day. During this period, many of our old beloved hymns were written. Still, prejudice and injustices remained.

For years after our Civil War, God poured out His blessings upon many nations, but again, they gradually wandered from His commandments. Our California gold rush ran rampant with greed, and the gay nineties of the 19th Century exposed new depths of decadence. During all their fervor for prosperity and frivolity, people forgot God. They were too busy clamoring for blessings; once again, Americans obsessed over idols and entertainment.

Then God raised another generation of preachers like Billy Sunday. Some Americans turned to God, but much of the nation continued on a destructive path, while a similar wave of moral recklessness swept Europe. Then World War I erupted. It became known as the "War to End All Wars." Some thought it might lead to permanent peace and prosperity.

After World War I, our nation prospered briefly, once again. These were the fun times of the Roaring '20s. However, people soon turned to lawlessness. In quick succession, within a 25-year period, we had World War I, our Great Depression and World War II. This era left the world's nations reeling from the cup of God's wrath.

Following World War II was one of the greatest revivals in America's history. God brought men like Billy Graham, Oral Roberts, Bill Bright and Kenneth Hagin. This was known as the

"Healing Revival" period, when God used more than 1,000 evangelists to bring healing to the nations. Great miracles occurred in America and throughout our world as God showed compassion and restoration. Once again, we see God's entire pattern: (1) rebellion, (2) invasion, (3) slavery, (4) repentance, (5) deliverance, (6) restoration, (7) peace.

America had rebelled in the 1920s. Then God allowed an economic invasion, as well as Hitler's invasion in Europe and the Japanese at Pearl Harbor. So America became enslaved to poverty and war. Then our great nation returned to God in repentance, and revival spread. God clearly repeats this pattern of judgment and restoration toward nations.

Though many people blame problems on current leaders, they don't realize we are simply reaping corrupt seeds of our past. In the 1990s, our nation, as a whole, drifted from God again. Many credited prosperity at that time to the government, blinded to the fact it also resulted from positive spiritual seeds sown in the past. It takes time for any seed, whether good or bad, to take root and grow.

Like God judged Israel by sending a Babylonian army to oppress them, so He will send America's enemies to inflict pain, until we repent of wickedness and return to Him. Many in our nation who are spiritually blind make excuses, blaming America's afflictions on administrations, enemies, nature, the religious right, the political left, and even God. Because they prefer darkness to light, people refuse to acknowledge truth. They refuse to concede the iniquities of our nation. Undiscerning people look to man's ingenuity to solve all our problems.

But if we fail to acknowledge God, we invite our own destruction like dozens of past civilizations. This principle remains throughout the centuries: *Our prosperity as a nation is in direct correlation to our obedience to God!*

The spiritual realm will always affect the natural realm. We have failed as a nation to give glory to God for our prosperity in the past. And it's a fact the spiritual seeds we sow now will take root and grow in the future, though in some cases we won't see the results until the next generation. But unless we repent as a nation, we'll continue to reap from corruption sown.

But we can postpone or prevent coming judgments on our nation by crying to God and returning to His Word, as Isaiah 55:7 says. If we humble ourselves and repent, God is faithful to comfort and restore, says Isaiah 1:26. Let's immediately begin to sow seeds of righteousness, like Proverbs 14:34 reminds us.

Deeds of Darkness Brought into Light

Starting with the new millennium, God began to uncover things hidden in darkness. America has seen evil brought out into the open.

> So do not be afraid of them. There is nothing concealed that will not be disclosed, or hidden that will not be made known.
> —Matthew 10:26

If not uncovered in this present life, all things will be uncovered at the Great Judgment in the future. But it's better they be uncovered and judged in this life than in the one to come. No area of life is untouched.

Sexual scandals with ministers and priests were brought into the open for all to see. We've seen corruption uncovered in our government and military. During the past decade God revealed dishonesty and greed of corporate executives. And we continue to see increasing moral depravity in Hollywood. Homosexuals demand special rights, without shame. Godless philosophies of many judges are clearly visible. Replacing truth and justice, they attempt to usurp the will of Americans and strip power from congress by making their own laws. Educators are hostile toward God and moral virtues.

All these arenas now display evil deeds and thoughts openly. But they existed in the 1990s also, hidden in darkness. Only believers full of His Spirit of Wisdom can see through their deception. Now, God has brought these wicked ways out into the open so everyone recognizes it. God has brought the American people to the valley of decision. Now, we must choose. Whom will you serve, God or man?

> Multitudes, multitudes in the valley of decision! For the day of the LORD is near in the valley of decision.
> —Joel 3:14

This is not a time for believers to fear or to be discouraged. It's a time for prayer and expectation. A nation's sins must be brought into the light for revival to come. God is revealing and tearing down corruption in America and planting seeds of righteousness.

"The ax is already at the root of the trees, and every tree that does not produce good fruit will be cut down and thrown into the fire," John the Baptist said in Luke 3:9.

There will be a season of repentance, sorrow, and soberness. But afterwards will be a time of great rejoicing. Thankfully, restoration always follows judgment!

> For his anger lasts only a moment, but his favor lasts a lifetime; weeping may remain for a night, but rejoicing comes in the morning.
> —Psalm 30:5

Christ Will Judge Nations

We are approaching the seven-year tribulation—a time of judgment like our world has never known! God will provide prophets who warn of these judgments, as God's ambassadors; they will speak to all nations. They will pluck-up and break down, destroy and overthrow, build and plant.

As in the past, God will give plenty of time to repent and return to Him. But the nations will refuse, because they love darkness rather than light, as scriptures say in Revelation 9:20-21 and 16:9-11. They will choose the path of lawlessness, bow to the beast, and esteem the Antichrist over our true Messiah. They will curse and blaspheme God as His cup of wrath pours upon the earth. Then Christ will return with his saints, in all His glory, to judge every living person.

> I saw heaven standing open and there before me was a white horse, whose rider is called Faithful and True. With justice he judges and makes war. His eyes are like blazing fire, and on his head are many crowns. He has a name written on him that no one knows but he himself. He is dressed in a robe dipped in blood, and his name is the Word of God. The armies of heaven were following him, riding on white horses and dressed in fine linen, white and clean. Out of his mouth comes a sharp sword with which to strike down the nations. "He will rule them with an iron scepter." He treads the winepress of the fury of the wrath of God Almighty. On his robe and on his thigh he has this name written: KING OF KINGS AND LORD OF LORDS.
>
> —Revelation 19:11-16

This time, God will not send plagues or an invading army. He will come Himself to execute judgment. He will come to the earth in power and great glory. Then every eye shall see Him. In the book of Isaiah, it tells how people will try to hide.

Men will flee to caves in the rocks and to holes in the ground from dread of the LORD and the splendor of his majesty, when he rises to shake the earth.
—Isaiah 2:19

Many people today flaunt their sins and persecute God's people, expecting this present life to last forever. Little do they realize the judgment to come. Then people persecuted for the name of Jesus will gather to execute judgment upon the earth with Him.

Revelation tells how kings will gather armies to war with Christ and His anointed. Can you imagine their rebellious audacity? And because each generation becomes more wicked, during the Great Tribulation many people will have absolutely no fear of God, though some will hide in fear. When wicked kings bring their armies to resist the Righteous One, God will speak one Word, and they will be destroyed. Then angels will call flesh-eating birds to feast, as shown in Revelation 19:17-18.

Afterward, God will comfort all nations and bring peace; war will cease. Lambs will sleep with lions, and children can play with snakes. For one thousand years peace and prosperity will flourish!

Our Messiah will rule and reign from Jerusalem. The new government will not be democratic, not subject to men's imperfections, so laws and policies will not change with public opinion. This earth will be ruled by the One who is perfect and just, and He will rule with a rod of iron.

> A shoot will come up from the stump of Jesse; from his roots a Branch will bear fruit. The Spirit of the LORD will rest on him—the Spirit of wisdom and of understanding, the Spirit of counsel and of power, the Spirit of knowledge and of the fear of the LORD—and he will delight in the fear of the LORD. He will not judge by what he sees with his eyes, or decide by what he hears with his ears; but with righteousness he will judge the

needy, with justice he will give decisions for the poor of the earth. He will strike the earth with the rod of his mouth; with the breath of his lips he will slay the wicked.

—Isaiah 11:1-4

Fruit Inspection

1. What is God's pattern to judge nations?

   _____
   _____
   _____
   _____

   Give examples:

   _____
   _____
   _____
   _____

   What pattern of judgment do you see in our nation?

   _____
   _____
   _____
   _____

2. List different principalities in this chapter who controlled nations.

   _____
   _____
   _____
   _____

What are their attributes?

What other controlling principalities aren't mentioned here?

3. What principalities will dominate during the Antichrist's reign?

4. What principality attempts to dominate our nation?

Describe its attributes:

5. How did the prophet Daniel overcome Persia's evil prince, in Daniel 10?

6. When the prophet Jeremiah warned of judgments on Judah, why did people refuse to believe him?

7. Since Jesus only did good, why did He pronounce judgment on Tyre, Sidon, and Capernaum?

   Matthew 11:20-24:

   Luke 10:13-15:

8. Why does God uncover evil deeds?

Matthew 10:26:

9. List how people will be deceived to take the mark of the beast.

10. When our Messiah returns to earth, how will He judge?

Revelation 19:15:

CHAPTER 7

THE FINAL CHAPTER
WHAT IS YOUR PART?

God's last judgment is at His Great White Throne. At this time, all those who ever existed will receive judgment, each according to their deeds. Then only people whose names are written in the Lamb's book of life will be spared eternal damnation.

> Then I saw a great white throne and him who was seated on it. Earth and sky fled from his presence, and there was no place for them. And I saw the dead, great and small, standing before the throne, and books were opened. Another book was opened, which is the book of life. The dead were judged according to what they had done as recorded in the books.
> —Revelation 20:11-12

God will soon finish writing the final chapter of this age. He is about to complete history (*His* story). God's list of believers bound for heaven is almost complete, called "The Lamb's book of life."

Most people enjoy stories with a happy ending. Have you ever read a book or watched a movie that ended in tragedy? Perhaps a main character was charismatic and heroic, so by the end you became emotionally attached, then saw them die. On occasion, I have left a theatre with my gut wrenched in grief, devastated over a main character in a needless tragedy.

As a five-year-old, I saw the Disney movie *Old Yeller,* which took place during our Civil War. The main character was a hound dog, and I was quite fond of animals, as most children are. As the story unfolded, I got emotionally attached to Old Yeller, who saved his owner from a wild animal attack but got bitten in the process, contracting rabies. Later, his master regretfully had to shoot him, the most merciful way to end a dog's suffering. I sat in the movie theater; tears streamed down my cheeks, while I hoped my sisters and friends didn't see me cry. However, Old Yeller had mated a female dog before he died, and his puppies were born after his death, so the story ended on a happy note.

It's true most people prefer to hear a story with a happy ending, especially when the story is about their own life. God wants each person's story to have a happy ending! God *wants* all of us to accept His Son's sacrifice and go to heaven!

But He will not violate our will. He wants everyone's name in the Lamb's book of life. But whether we are in the book is our choice. If we overcome evil through faith in Jesus' saving death and resurrection, our name will be placed in God's book, so we'll live an eternal, happy life.

> He who overcomes will, like them, be dressed in white. I will never blot out his name from the book of life, but will acknowledge his name before my Father and his angels.
> —Revelation 3:5

Is your name written in God's book? We have the God-given ability to choose to believe Christ for salvation. Then God gives us the privilege to write our own life's story. What will we write? Will our story end well? Will we write about a life of obedience and surrender to Christ? Will we produce good fruit for His kingdom? Or will we write about a life of sin and rebellion?

God desires to write a book of eternal glory for each of us, but in omniscience, He knows many will reject His love and plan for their life. We each need to ask, will I receive His wonderful story of love and blessings for my life?

God gives us breath, then the choice to write our story, abilities to fulfill our destiny. He even gave us guidelines to live, in the Bible. If we live by faith in Christ, we receive peace and joy, then eternal life. But anyone who writes their life's story with rebellion, rejecting Christ and His commandments, will not have their name written in God's book of Life. They will still be judged at His Great White Throne, then totally separated from Him—forever!

> If anyone's name was not found written in the book of life, he was thrown into the lake of fire.
> —Revelation 20:15

Road to Victory

In the November 2004 American election, one candidate had a campaign slogan: "Road to Victory." In the Kingdom of God there is also a road to victory. It is the straight and narrow road, which leads to life.

> Enter through the narrow gate. For wide is the gate and broad is the road that leads to destruction, and many enter through it. But small is the gate and narrow the road that leads to life, and only a few find it.
> —Matthew 7:13-14

Our journey down the straight and narrow lasts a lifetime. As disciples of Jesus Christ, we are merely sojourners in this present world. "This world is not our home," as an old country hymn says. Life's journey is miniscule in light of a vast eternity. Sadly, much of the world takes a wide road, which leads to destruction, as Proverbs 14:12 says.

Why is the road to victory so narrow in the Kingdom of God? Why do few find this way to victory? Why is the way of destruction so wide?

Many people fail to enter the straight gate because they are asleep to spiritual reality. But we know the spiritual realm affects the natural realm, which is temporary, while the spiritual is eternal. Yet people still only see what's in front of their noses and never give eternity a thought! Of course the wide road of destruction meets less resistance from the world. It appears easy, full of comforts, but it still leads to destruction. People do not realize they need a Savior when they live for satisfaction from carnal materialism alone. They live blind and ignorant of coming destruction!

On the other hand, the prince of darkness attempts to resist those who choose the narrow way. To a simpleton, the straight path appears uncomfortable. Persecution, sacrifice, surrender, and obedience all seem unappealing. However, the narrow path leads to peace, joy, and eternal life, but it is traveled by faith.

Jesus is the straight gate, and He is the narrow way. Eternal life is exclusively available through Him. He is our road to victory, which is so simple, yet few find it, as John 14:6 tells us.

Five common reasons exist why people avoid the narrow way. First, many don't know how to merge onto the road. They have never heard the gospel of Jesus Christ. Second, others know how, but refuse to travel it; because they love the dark street they're on, rather than one with bright light.

> For God did not send his Son into the world to condemn the world, but to save the world through him. Whoever believes in him is not condemned, but whoever does not believe stands condemned already because he has not believed in the name of

> God's one and only Son. This is the verdict: Light has come into the world, but men loved darkness instead of light because their deeds were evil.
> —John 3:17-19

Third, people might enter the straight path, but get distracted by interests on the world's side streets. They assume wealth and the possessions it buys will fulfill their spirit, so they exit onto a detour.

Fourth, some are offended by possible persecution, so they return to the broad road that leads to destruction, never braving the new journey.

Many people believe they are already on the road of victory. However, they continue powerless, blinded by our deceitful world and its master of darkness. They may attend church services and claim to know God. Yet, their lives and deeds show the opposite.

Like Jesus' parable in Matthew 13:24-30, these people are weeds mixed in fields of valuable wheat. They might even believe their evil deeds are unseen. They simply don't realize God spares them so the wheat is not damaged if He tried to immediately uproot the weeds. Nevertheless, there is coming a day when good and bad will get separated. Worthless tares will get cut down and burned in everlasting fire, while mature wheat will be harvested for eternal life, as the parable describes.

Finally, millions of kind, helpful people expect to enter heaven because of their good works, their righteousness, apart from Christ. Because they don't look into the spiritual mirror of the Bible, they don't see their sins, how they fall short of God's standards. They are deceived to believe that doing good deeds will earn their way to heaven.

Others are self-righteous hypocrites. Those who believe this great lie see everyone else's shortcomings but remain blind to their own. They look on others with arrogant disdain and deadly motives then show an outward appearance of righteousness. Jesus called them Pharisees.

Religious Pharisees were too prideful to admit any wrong. We see this same erroneous thought in many world religions. They attempt to please God by their own efforts and righteousness, while selectively ignoring commands.

These key principles show us how to enter onto the narrow road and stay there, to attain life:

1. Godly Sorrow: A conviction of our sins (2 Corinthians 7:10)
2. Repentance: Willing to humble ourselves and change (Acts 2:37-38)
3. Faith: Belief in our Lord Jesus Christ without seeing; Trust (Acts 16:31)
4. Forgiveness: Receive forgiveness of sins by faith (Acts 13:38)
   Learn to forgive others (Mark 11:25-26)
5. Seek: To press on to know Jesus Christ (Philippians 3:10-14)
   Study and meditate in the Bible (Psalm 1:1-2)
   Spend time in prayer and worship (1 Thessalonians 5:17; Romans 12:1)
6. Filled with His Spirit: To wait on the Lord, receive power from Him (Ephesians 5:18-20)
7. Endurance: Never give up. Stay on the narrow road until the end (Revelation 2:25-26)

Jesus is the Great Fruit Inspector. He will return soon to inspect His garden. When the Son of Man returns, as Luke 18:8 states, will He find faith on our earth? Will His trees produce good fruit? Will he know us as His own? When He comes to inspect, will He find we produce good fruit?

The Great Fruit Inspector never makes a mistake. Nothing slips by Him unnoticed, whether good or bad—ever! He knows what is in the hearts of men, women, and children.

Mankind's final chapter is almost finished. The final chapter of our life speeds nearer, daily. Even if we live more than one hundred years, it is like a grain of sand on the earth compared to the length of eternity.

If we fall under God's future judgment, it won't be His fault. He loves each of us and desires we spend eternity with Him. It's His very nature of love that gives us freedom to choose. It's also His nature of love that brings judgment, now and in our future. Without judgment, God's whole creation could plummet to anarchy and total destruction. Love contains justice, as well as mercy, truth, and grace.

We can ensure our name is written in the Lamb's book of Life. We can avoid judgments to come. Instead of fear and dread, we can live each day with confident expectation, with peace and joy. We can have life—today, and happily ever after.

Jesus wants our name in His book of life. He is the road to victory. He is the Great Fruit Inspector. Jesus knocks at the door of our heart, offering the gift of repentance, salvation, and deliverance, as Revelation 3:19:20 says. We can receive His gift of eternal life through faith, or reject Him.

What will you choose?

> "This day I call heaven and earth as witnesses against you that I have set before you life and death, blessings and curses. Now choose life, so that you and your children may live."
> —Deuteronomy 30:19

Final Inspection

1. What is the narrow way that leads to life?

   _____
   _____
   _____

   What is the broad way that leads to destruction?

   _____
   _____
   _____

2. Why did Jesus call the way to life narrow?

   _____
   _____
   _____

   Give reasons why few will find it:

   _____
   _____
   _____

3. List key principals required to enter the narrow way of life:

   _____
   _____
   _____

4. Is your name written in the Lamb's book of life?
   _____
   _____
   _____
   _____

5. How can we have eternal life?
   _____
   _____
   _____
   _____

6. What is your purpose on this earth?
   _____
   _____
   _____
   _____

7. How can we be spared from judgments to come?
   _____
   _____
   _____
   _____

Appendix 1

THE TRUTH WILL MAKE YOU FREE!

November 19, 1999
Dear Friends,

We hope everyone is well and prospering as we near a new millennium. God's timetable continues to move forward. He will bring His word and plans to pass. But we can choose to ignore Him, go about our own routine, and miss what He has planned for us. For the righteous, He plans wonderful things. For the wicked, it's fearful judgment.

As this age draws to a close, we can sense the urgency of the times—if we listen to His voice. It's our responsibility to find out what our part is in His plan then do it, whether it is prayer, giving, teaching, doing good deeds, or whatever He tells us.

Our desire is to lead our family and friends into a deeper walk with our Messiah. No one has arrived in knowing all truth, because God's truth is unlimited. There is always more. He desires us to love truth and hate evil! But there's a great void of truth in our world today, which is why evil abounds, and people pursue only what they love. God talks about this selfishness:

> For the secret power of lawlessness is already at work; but the one who now holds it back will continue to do so till he is taken out of the way. And then the lawless one will be revealed, whom the Lord Jesus will overthrow with the breath of his mouth and destroy by the splendor of his coming. The coming of the lawless one will be in accordance with the work of Satan displayed in all kinds of counterfeit miracles, signs and wonders, and in every sort of evil that deceives those who are perishing. They perish because they refused to love the truth and so be saved. For this reason God sends them a powerful delusion so that they will believe the lie and so that all will be condemned who have not believed the truth but have delighted in wickedness.
> —2 Thessalonians 2:7-12

We, as children of God, must continue to seek His truth, love the Lord with all our heart, mind and strength, and burn continually with His zeal. If we don't love correction and reproof from His Word, then we probably don't love His truth. God's truth is the *only* way to live a life of joy and freedom.

Jesus said, "You shall know the truth, and the truth shall make you free." His disciples had a focus: to learn God's truth and teach it to others. We hope these words encourage you also, as you continue to seek God's truth.

We are busy with jobs, school, church, etc. For the past year, Gaby translated material from the children's ministry of our church into Spanish, to distribute throughout South and Central America. Please continue to pray for us, if the Holy Spirit should lay us on your heart.

Yours in Christ,
Steve and Gaby Carney

Appendix 2

THE TRUTH WILL MAKE YOU FREE!

September 23, 2001
Dear Friends,

As you may remember, I felt led to write a short letter at the turn of this century, about what the Spirit of the Lord was revealing, concerning the last days. I mentioned the turn of this century ushered in what the Apostle Paul called "The Spirit of Lawlessness." Many people's hearts today are so hardened they are unable to discern good and evil. God revealed to me that because of this lawlessness and people despising His truth, this century would be one of judgments. Consider the Word of the Lord:

> Now, brothers, about times and dates we do not need to write to you, for you know very well that the day of the Lord will come like a thief in the night. While people are saying, "Peace and safety," destruction will come on them suddenly, as labor pains on a pregnant woman, and they will not escape. But you, brothers, are not in darkness so that this day should surprise you like a thief. You are all sons of the light and sons of the day. We do not

belong to the night or to the darkness. So then, let us not be like others, who are asleep, but let us be alert and self-controlled.
—I Thessalonians 5:1-6

John 16:12-13 says, "I have much more to say to you, more than you can now bear. But when he, the Spirit of truth, comes, he will guide you into all truth. He will not speak on his own; he will speak only what he hears, and he will tell you what is yet to come."

The key from these scriptures is, "he will tell you what is yet to come." But He will only show those who have his indwelling Spirit, and those who are willing to spend time with him, listening to every word, esteeming it with respect.

I feel some believers knew judgment was coming upon New York City before September 11, 2001. These believers, although deeply grieved over the suffering, were not shocked or caught off-guard. And I must confess to you that I repented for not praying for our nation as I should have. The week before the terrible incident, my wife and I both had trouble sleeping, for no known reason.

> Now there were some present at that time who told Jesus about the Galileans whose blood Pilate had mixed with their sacrifices. Jesus answered, "Do you think that these Galileans were worse sinners than all the other Galileans because they suffered this way? I tell you, no!
>
> But unless you repent, you too will all perish. Or those eighteen who died when the tower in Siloam fell on them—do you think they were guiltier than all the others living in Jerusalem? I tell you, no!
>
> But unless you repent, you too will all perish." Then he told this parable: "A man had a fig tree, planted in his vineyard, and he went to look for fruit on it, but did not find any. So he said to the man who took care of the vineyard, 'For three years now I've

been coming to look for fruit on this fig tree and haven't found any. Cut it down! Why should it use up the soil?'

'Sir,' the man replied, 'Leave it alone for one more year, and I'll dig around it and fertilize it. If it bears fruit next year, fine! If not, then cut it down.'"

—Luke 13:1-9

This is what Jesus teaches His Church concerning the Twin Towers disaster. It's not that these people were worse than any of the rest of us. We must all repent, put Christ first in our lives, and bear fruit for his kingdom. But He said the only way we can produce fruit is to abide or live with him. We are His branches, but without the vine, we dry up, becoming useless for his kingdom. This is what opens us to influence from the enemy of darkness.

About three years ago I was reading the Bible from the software on my computer. As I browsed through the Scriptures, I felt led to the story about Noah's ark. So I read through it quickly, wanting to go to Psalms, one of my favorite books. But my computer froze at the scriptures in Genesis.

I read it again more slowly and felt an impression that God was trying to tell me something very important. So I read these passages a third time.

God, what are you saying? I thought to myself. After waiting in reverence for a few minutes, His answer began to come:

The end of the period of grace is drawing to a close. God's judgments will gradually increase each year and decade as this dispensation comes to a conclusion. We, the Church of Jesus Christ, are to prepare an ark for our family, a refuge from coming storms.

You may think, *How do we prepare an ark?* I asked the same question. The ark foreshadows Christ. It gave salvation. We are to enter into God's presence by the blood of Jesus Christ. We must set aside time to spend with him in fellowship, studying His Word, worshipping, and praying. We should do this alone and as a family, and by attending church.

We also need to lose our lives daily for the Kingdom of God, denying our own fleshly desires for pleasure and comfort, so we are led by His Spirit. As we do, we will become more aware of His presence. When we eat, sleep, and work, His presence will fill us. In His presence is fullness of joy, and we can hear His voice.

As we abide in Him, He'll shield us from danger. He will reveal things in us that need changing. So as we judge ourselves and mature, we'll be spared judgment.

He will also reveal to us things to come, so we won't be completely taken off-guard, but we'll know what to do. And we won't fear bad news.

Psalm 91:1 says, "He who dwells in the shelter of the Most High will rest in the shadow of the Almighty." This is the only way to get protection from coming judgments.

I believe there will be one more final revival upon the earth before the Great Tribulation spoken of in Daniel and Revelation. However, even during this revival, God's judgments will also increase. May you surrender your life to Jesus Christ. I pray you will run to the Ark and enter its safety, and that you will invite—rather compel—others into the Ark!

Sincerely,
Steve Carney

ENDNOTES

Chapter 2

[1] Henry Bosley Woolf, et al., Eds. *Webster's New Collegiate Dictionary,* 8th ed., (Springfield, Massachusetts: G. & C. Merriam Co., 1975), p. 1302.

[2] Rick Warren, *The Purpose Driven Life*, (Grand Rapids, Michigan: Zondervan, 2002), p.197.

Chapter 3

[1] Jordan S. Rubin, *The Maker's Diet*, (Lake Mary, Florida: Strang Communication, 2004), p. 156-157.

[2] Warren, p.194.

[3] Woolf, et al., **Webster's New Collegiate Dictionary**, 8th ed., p. 626.

[4] Matthew Henry (1706), "Mathew Henry Complete Commentary," *The Bible Collection Deluxe* (Computer software), Waconia, MN: ValuSoft, 2002.

Chapter 4

[1] Smith Wigglesworth, *Smith Wigglesworth on Healing*, (New Kensington, PA: Whitaker House, 1999), p.17.

Chapter 5

[1] Alfred Rahlfs, et al., eds., "The Wisdom of Solomon," *Good News Bible With Deuterocanonicals/Apocrypha: Today's English Version* (New York: American Bible Society, 1992), p.893.

Pleasant Word

To order additional copies of this title call:
1-877-421-READ (7323)
or please visit our Web site at
www.pleasantwordbooks.com

If you enjoyed this quality custom-published book,
drop by our Web site for more books and information.

www.winepressgroup.com
"Your partner in custom publishing."

Printed in the United States
116202LV00005B/163-297/P